A Gift of Quilts

A Cultural Olympiad Inspire Mark Project

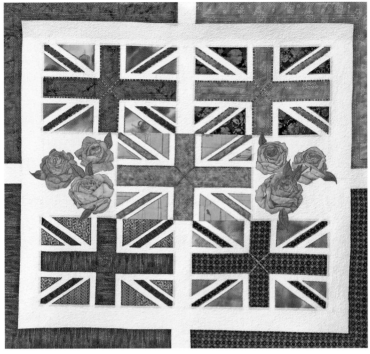

"Flags & Roses", Patricia Collinson

Published by Traplet Publications Limited 2012
Traplet House,
Pendragon Close,
Malvern,
Worcestershire. WR14 1GA
United Kingdom.

ISBN 978-1-907712-08-1

T R A P L E T
P U B L I C A T I O N S

Printed by Warners, Bourne, Lincolnshire

A Gift of Quilts
Contents

Quilts presented to Great Britain at the 1996 Olympic Games. Atlanta

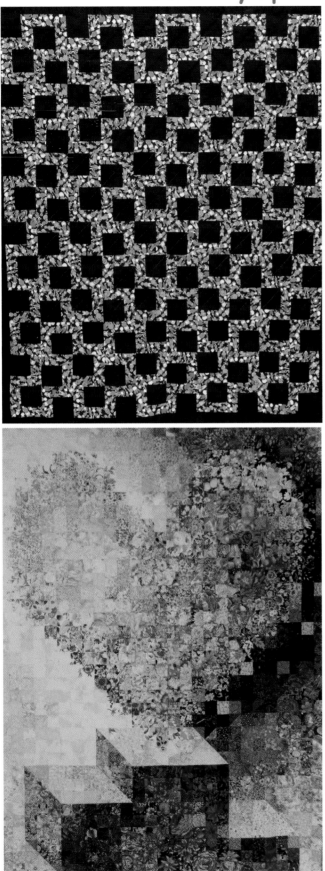

Sir Steve Redgrave CBE

Richard Palmer CBE

Kaffe Fassett -
A Gift of Quilts' Patron

What a bizarre art patchwork is when you look at it objectively. We quilt makers buy and collect fabric, which we cut into various shapes and then sew together. I suddenly saw how strange it could look when commissioning a new artist to design fabric for our range. He was a rug designer so was used to sprawling designs in beautiful pallets of wine tones and leafy greens. We had to explain that everything he painted for us would have to be cut up in 1 to 10 inch pieces - a strange brief for an artist.

But we patchworkers, like our mosaic making cousins, delight in the combining of unlikely patterns and fragments of colour. The same delight a child has with a bowl full of buttons, beads or puzzle shapes.

Then there is the craft of precise cutting and sewing which has inspired a brilliantly efficiency of tools and methods that patchworkers pass on to each other. In my experience, it is the most generous craft in the decorative arts world for sharing of fabric and expertise.

What is most amazing, but totally understandable to me is the success of the shops in this dire economic climate. The deep satisfaction and comfort people gain from making things with their hands – particularly sewing - is proved by the reports we get from sewing shops all over the world. I have just been to the Houston Quilt Festival and Birmingham Quilt Festival where excited quilters from all over the world were thronging to see displays of quilts and shop for the materials to make more as well as taking workshops and attending talks on the subject. A passionate quest for learning and sharing this creative pastime.

In this book we have some of the results of that passion. One of the best aspects of this craft is the makers can sew warmth and affection into a tangible complex cloth to give (what a powerful word and act) to another to enhance their lives. I can think of few more satisfying acts than spending time making a beautiful object for someone you love or admire from afar.

We who have stitched, like to be admired for our work, but have already reaped our reward from the hours of quiet creativity. In this book we see our craft meet the world of sport at its most noble. This is another proud group of people who devote time and intelligence to refining their skills. Quilters salute them with these gifts from their hands.

Kaffe Fassett

Kaffe Fassett

The Authors

Sharon Garrick

Sharon Garrick has been involved in the world of patchwork and quilting for nearly thirty years. Sharon trained as a commercial artist specialising in printing and package design but soon found that working with textiles gave her more freedom for colour and design.

As an active member of The Quilters Guild of the British Isles Sharon has been involved in organising many quilting exhibitions and patchwork events. In recent years these have included the 'Spirit of Sarum' exhibition at the Salisbury and South Wiltshire Museum and 'Project Alzheimer's' at Sarum College, both in Salisbury, Wiltshire. Project Alzheimer's was a weekend show of Journal quilts made and donated to raise funds for the local branch of the Alzheimer's Society. Such was the success of this event that Sharon was able to hand over £4000 to the society in memory of her late mother, Sheila.

Sharon is a published author writing for several patchwork magazines and she has also produced a booklet of quilting patterns from the Reserve collection of the Salisbury Museum using her drawing skills to recreate the motifs from the stored garments. She has written all the articles and press releases for A Gift of Quilts and created and maintains the project web site.

As well as working with Jenny Rundle on A Gift of Quilts Sharon is an experienced teacher with regular classes in Wiltshire and the surrounding areas.

Jenny Rundle

For more than thirty years Jenny Rundle has made patchwork quilts, taught patchwork techniques and also ran a successful patchwork & quilting shop, staying in contact with many of her old customers from across the world. She has had her work exhibited in this country, Europe, USA, and Japan including several one-man exhibitions. Jenny works both by hand and machine stitching but her love is hand stitching, often making a top in a matter of days. Jenny's first quilt was to finish a hexagon quilt started by her sister but her work has evolved over the years from using traditional patchwork blocks to varying traditional designs to now designing her own work and expanding on techniques that she loves and imparts to others at workshops. Jenny has developed interests in beading, weaving & different forms of rag rug making putting her fabric scraps to good use. Jenny belongs to the Tiddly Dyke Quilters, Test Valley Quilters & the KISS group and with Sharon is also involved in organising Quilting Days for up to 100 quilters for which she designs and produces packs used in the mystery workshops, ranging from tea-towel bags to Valentine's Day gifts. She has been an active Quilters Guild member both locally and nationally for over 25 years both on committees and organising events. Jenny is currently working on a new book of Art Nouveau designs using hand and machine appliqué.

A Gift of Quilts
The Project

A Gift of Quilts is a showcase to the world of patchwork and quilting in the British Isles today. Historically quilting in the British Isles can be traced back to as far as the thirteenth century, when quilting was used in protective garments worn under or over armour or chain mail and as such it can be said that quilting is one of the oldest traditional crafts in the British Isles. References to bed quilts can be found in the 15th century Account Rolls of the Priory of Durham. Quilting reached its zenith in the seventeenth and eighteenth centuries when it was used in the fashionable costumes and quilting was combined with patchwork, but in the nineteenth century the two went out of favour as factory made bedcovers were more plentiful and cheaper. Quilting, however survived by being passed down from mother to daughter, in cottages, farmhouses and colliery villages, which were immune from the world of fashion due to their isolated locations and distance from shops that sold the new factory made bedcovers. Quilting continued mainly in the North and South West of England and in parts of Wales, Scotland and Ireland, with some of these areas regarding quilting as the finer art to patchwork. During the nineteenth century quilting was becoming recognised as a craft by the Arts and Crafts movement and examples were on show at many exhibitions. During the first years of the Twentieth century the craft suffered a decline but quilting still survived in the North of England with some quilters working on a self-employed basis or through the Rural Industries Bureau. The Women's Institute also maintained interest in the craft and if it were not for the dedication of women, which included Amy Emms MBE, Avril Colby & Mavis Fitzrandolph patchwork and quilting would not be where it is today. Quilting would not just be seen as a revival but as a new and vigorous phase in a truly British tradition, with modern quilt makers deriving inspiration from the experiences of their forebears and adapting the old ways to their own designs.

The Olympic Games and Paralympics (The Games) are both major international events featuring summer and winter sports, in which thousands of athletes participate in a variety of multi-sport competitions. The Games have come to be regarded as the world's foremost sporting competition with more than 250 nations participating and are held every four years. The Paralympics are held immediately following their respective Olympic Games. The Olympic Games are for able-bodied athletes whilst the Paralympics for those athletes with a physical disability including mobility disability, amputations, blindness and Cerebral Palsy.

The Special Olympics is the world's largest sports organization for children and adults with intellectual disabilities or ID. The Special Olympics is for people who are different because they learn new skills slowly. They may not understand ideas that other people learn easily and they are different in other ways as well. Alternating between summer and winter, the Special Olympics World Games are held every four years with participants from more than 175 countries.

When the announcement was made in July 2005 that London had won the bid to stage the 2012 Olympic Games & Paralympics the authors being quilt makers of many years experience felt that the making and giving of quilts would be a wonderful way of sharing the UK's heritage with the world; little did they realise the enormous task facing them. Many people would never be able to take part in the Games themselves and the project was a good way of getting them involved, this could be achieved by making quilts to be presented as gifts from the people of the UK to the countries attending The Games in London. Research found that countries participating in the Games traditionally received a welcome bag, miniature mascot, or a souvenir medal from the host country but at the 1996 Atlanta Olympic Games two quilts had been presented to each country: one went to the flag-bearer, the other to the head Olympic official for that country. No reference could be found of gift presentations being made to athletes or officials at previous Paralympics and it was decided to present one quilt to each country participating at both the 2012 Olympic Games and Paralympics. The project was off the ground but it needed a name, looking through the book of the Atlanta quilts there were several references to "The Gift of Quilts", the project now had a name. How many quilts did the project need? Exact numbers of countries attending The Games is not known until the year of The Games, so a little guess work was required, so by looking back at the number of countries attending previous Games and adding a little, 500 quilts became the figure. What size should the quilts be? The minimum size was set at one metre square (40" x 40") with a maximum size of 137cm x 198cm (54" x 78") single bed size.

Over many months during 2008 & 2009, letters were sent to the London Organising Committee of the Olympic Games (LOCOG), all Local Authorities in the United Kingdom, women's organisations, including articles for all craft magazines and various craft guilds including the Women's Institute and The Quilters Guild of the British Isles.

Encouraging responses came back and at the 2009 Festival of Quilts the project went live. Textile Artist Kaffe Fassett agreed to be the projects Patron, Kaffe has inspired thousands of people across the world with his colourful work in patchwork, fabric, knitting, needlepoint, painting and mosaics and the project was honoured to have him aboard. Brandon Mably who manages Kaffe's Studio in London and is a designer in his own right assisted Kaffe as Patron. Subsequently in 2010 the project applied for and became part of The London 2012 Cultural Olympiad, which is the largest cultural celebration in the history of the modern Olympic and the Paralympic Movements and is designed to give everyone in the UK a chance to be part of London 2012 and inspire creativity across all forms of culture. The project was granted the Inspire Mark as a non-commercial organisation genuinely inspired by the London 2012 Games. It did, however mean that we could not have sponsorship or support from a commercial organisation and that the project would have to raise all funds needed.

The project asked people to register their intention to make and donate a quilt, each quilt being registered and given a number, this allowed the team to see how near the target figure of quilts required they were. Initially at the start of 2010 progress was slow but following the Quilters Guild of the British Isles AGM held at Southport and the Festival of Quilts the registration numbers jumped to over 450 and 500 was reached by December 2010.

Quilts were being registered by individuals, groups of friends, patchwork & quilting groups, Women's Institute groups, Over 60's clubs, schools, Guide and Brownie packs, prison hand-craft groups, U3A groups, retirement home craft groups, charity workers and many more too numerous to mention.

Quilts are considered a feminine art, in that most quilt makers have traditionally been women. But men have always sewn and made quilts, Joseph Hedley being one, Joe the Quilter as he was known even had verses written about him by A Wright and these form part of the folklore of the North of England today. Some of the quilts received by the project have been made by men; seek them out in the photographs of the quilts.

The quilts needed to be labelled as the team knew it was important that every quilt should have one, not just in case the quilt went missing but because each quilt tells a story about the person or persons who made it. An anonymous quilt is missing a vital piece of the story: a label sewn on the reverse of the quilt gives the name(s) of the maker(s), their address and most importantly the title of the quilt, which gives an immediate link from the maker to the person receiving the quilt.

Quilts started to arrive in 2010 and could initially be stored on beds but the team quickly realised that this could not be a permanent solution and subsequently a storage facility was found that was dry, secure and let at a reasonable rent. Two 4ft by 8ft racking units were erected, each having 4 shelves, which could hold up to 50 quilts each. Fund-raising was started, initially raffles and tombola's but most funds came from a £1 Fabric Lucky Dip, and fabric being donated by individuals and companies, in this way over £4000 was raised.

The authors wanted not only the makers to see their quilts on display but also to showcase British patchwork & quilting to the world and an exhibition was held at Olympia II, London as part of the 2012 Stitch & Craft Show, the only time all the quilts would be seen before going to their recipient countries.

Over 10,000 people have taken part in "A Gift of Quilts" and have ranged in age from nine years to ninety to encompass all ages, race, gender, background, disability, sexuality, religion and abilities and represents a wide cross-section of the peoples of the United Kingdom. Their legacy to the world is one of colour, and design; the tactile feel of cloth. Those taking part have spent many hours choosing their design, sourcing the fabrics. Planning, cutting, stitching, embellishing and quilting a piece of work that is a very personal gift to a country. They have taken part in a project that has enabled so many of them to be a part of the great organisation that is The Olympic Games & Paralympics and to feel a sense of pride that is alongside those who step on the podium to receive their medals.

The legacy of "A Gift of Quilts" is one that will take quilts from the people of the United Kingdom around the whole world. "A Gift of Quilts" has brought together people who might never have sewn, who now have a new group of friends to meet with and share a common bond. Those who had difficulty having their voices heard might now have a creative outlet that enables then to reach out to all corners of the community. Some who may have physical disabilities have also been part of a colourful, dynamic process linked to The Games and feel included when they might have been previously denied.

Our website www.agiftofquilts.co.uk was viewed by over 8,000 people, thank you to all who supported us and took part in "A Gift of Quilts"

Jenny & Sharon

Quilt Snippets

Quilt 148
Jenny Hornsey, of Basingstoke, contacted A Gift of Quilts as she wished to make a quilt for the Olympics in memory of her father, Ralph D Binfield. Mr Binfield wrote a book "The Story of the Olympic Games" in 1948 (published by the Oxford University Press). He also represented Great Britain in the Arts Competition at the London Olympics in 1948 with a Narrative Poem about the first marathon.

Quilt 113
The quilt is called 'Free Running London' which represents both the liberating quality of sport and also the freedom which the Tube lines and the act of meandering give us to explore the city. I am almost reluctant to part with my Gift of a Quilt but am also thrilled that it will be heading to a new home as a symbol of friendship. I hope the quilt is enjoyed, used, cuddled or inspires others to produce their own. A quilt is not a quilt if it does not have the companionship of people.

Quilt 123
I was excited to hear the Olympics would be in London in 2012 and would love to be involved. I would not be able to visit the Olympic Park, become a volunteer or attend the events. I could however make a quilt and so feel a part of the Games.

Quilt 133
This quilt was made by the staff, students and friends of Chace Community School. The group had a wide variety of experience in sewing and patchwork – some had none – you will notice the different 'styles' of stitches used!

Quilt 152
"Our husbands can not understand why we buy fabric, cut it up and sew it back together again. We can understand perfectly well!"

Quilt 156
This quilt was hand stitched in a prison cell by Bob Anderton. He was also able to use a sewing machine in the prison workshop to complete the quilt. Bob is a member of the Fine Cell Work team of inmates and was inspired to make this quilt after he had seen pictures of the Gee's Bend quilts.

Quilt 165
Members of the Nythe Patchwork and Quilting group used fabrics from their personal stashes and various collections of materials for their quilt. "We loved the bright cheerful effect and feel it reflects the fun and enjoyment we had making this quilt; hence the name "Bright Delight".

Quilt 167
"My quilt represents a door to the future. The sunrise at the top of the quilt suggests there is always hope to fulfil your dreams and the possibility for a better life."

Quilt 182
"I have made this quilt because it would be an opportunity for me to be involved in the Games of 2012, particularly as I am not an athlete!"

Quilt 260
The Wednesday Patchers from Dorchester have made their quilt to depict all the wonders of the British seaside. Sidney Francis, a relative of a group member, carried the Olympic Torch in Torquay for the 1948 Olympic Games.

Quilt 265
'A couple of years ago Sharon Garrick was a guest speaker for Wessex Quiltmakers at one of our regular evening meetings. She led a mini-workshop based on her own 'Hand of Friendship' quilt. We had such fun and when a Gift of Quilts was launched we decided to put our 'hands' to good use by making two group quilts for the Olympic project. The results are 'Hands around the World' and 'Hands of Friendship'. Our thanks go to Sharon and her colleagues for all their inspiration and for working so tirelessly for A Gift of Quilts.'

Quilt 268
Ladies of Pontypridd Women's Institute made a quilt showing the Layers and Landmarks of Wales. The Welsh countryside and the Welsh language are synonymous. They are essential ingredients of our uniqueness. The words on the blocks were chosen by WI members – some a reference to the spirit of the Olympic Games, others relate to the features of Pontypridd.

Quilt 274
By emailing photographs to one computer and then printing the images onto fabric we brought together modern technology and traditional design to create a pictorial quilt of our village of Womborne, Dorset.

Quilt 307
Made as a memorial to my father P.F De Boerr. He was a very talented swimmer and took part in selection trials for the Olympic swimming team or he might in fact have taken part in the Olympic swimming competition. Unfortunately I don't know which Olympics that might have been. However, his love of swimming has been passed on to me and in turn I have shared this with my family.

Quilt 344
"I made this quilt 'Flaming Stars' for the 2012 Olympic Games, and although I cannot attend the Games, my quilt can!!!"

Quilt 356
By participating in the Olympic Games we encourage the freedom to make friends and bring peace through understanding more of other cultures. This Dove of Peace and Friendship wreath is symbolic of all that.

Quilt 389
Since that day in 2005 when we were first awarded the Olympics, a lot has changed; for the world, for this country and for me personally. Sometimes it may seem that the world has gone crazy, but 2012 offers us the chance to throw aside political, social and economic differences as the pride of our nations battle it out to be the best they can be. This is the greatest show on earth. This quilt has allowed me to become part of such an occasion. With the stitches that I have worked I can become part of the history of this country, the Olympics and of the world. I can look back and say I took part. Now that is a gift to me!

Quilt 465
A quilt made by students with learning difficulties and disabilities from Brockenhurst College in the New Forest, Hampshire shows the forest through the seasons. The Attic Window design has 56 windows each with a different view.

Quilt 467
Pam Hyams and daughter Rachel Sharpe had family members involved in the Olympics. An uncle, Roy Matthews MBE was a British Champion Archer, Grand Master Bowman and a member of the 1972 Munich Olympics team. His wife, Mary Matthews MBE was with the British Olympic Archery team for 15 years and team manager from 1971-1981. They both received their MBE's for services to Archery (not usual for a married couple to both be honoured this way!)

Quilt 472
"The title 'London Challenge' was chosen because it was a challenge in the first instance to make our quilt and we feel the Olympics is the greatest of all athletic challenges."

Quilt 479
My inspiration was to be the maker of one of over 400 quilts travelling to every corner of the globe. I found an old traditional pattern called "Trellis" then pieced and hand quilted a colourful lap quilt that would act as a reminder of a fantastic 2012 Olympic Games held in England.

Quilt 480
Peter Simpson, aged 74, made a quilt whose concept was "green". The front of the quilt is made exclusively of men's old ties. "All the fabrics used were materials that would probably have been thrown away. I was inspired by the thought that somebody, somewhere, involved in the 2012 Olympics would have a unique reminder of The Games."

Behind The Scenes

Quilt 120
This quilt features items that are typical of the area in which we live - Norfolk. We have many windmills and a long coast line that has lighthouses and beach huts. We hope this quilt reflects aspects of Norfolk and will make the recipients want to find out more about our rural county.

Quilt 126
"Something from Everyone" by Basingstoke and Old Basing U3A, is a mixture of traditional blocks with the emblems of the Home Counties in the centre.

Quilt 14
This quilt by the Baker Street Babes is all about the British weather. One of the most talked about topics of conversation amongst friends and visitors to this island.

Quilt 131
"Whitstable by the sea" was inspired by this seaside town in Kent. It depicts the shoreline that includes boats, seagulls and beach huts.

Quilt 25
The Oakwood Quilters have featured a blend of traditional Thanksgiving and modern day Derbyshire Heritage found throughout the Derbyshire Dales in their quilt.

Quilt 34
Images of Windsor Castle, Tower Bridge, the Spinnaker Tower, King Alfred (King of Wessex) and the Needles of the Isle of Wight give this quilt a truly British flavour.

Quilt 61
In their quilt "Circles and London Icons" Liz McKeown and friends capture the Olympic Spirit.

Quilt 135
"The Raven". When John Flamsteed, the astronomical observer of Charles II, 1630-1685, tried to take measurements from the White Tower he encountered interference from ravens who lived amongst the Tower's towers. He appealed to the king who ordered the ravens killed. However, someone unknown warned Charles that should all the ravens ever leave, the White Tower would fall, and with it the British monarchy and kingdom. Charles, or whoever really did first hear about the legend, evidently believed it, for it was ordered that six ravens were to be kept at the Tower at all times.

Quilt 115
A lucky find of the map of the world enabled the Rainbows (girls aged 5-6), Brownies (girls aged 7-10) and Guides (girls aged 10-14) of West Horndon to design, with the help of their Guiders, a quilt which would depict the global spirit of the Games and echo the Guiding movement which is active in so many countries of the world. For some girls it was their first opportunity to use a sewing machine. The Guiders hope it will inspire them to take up sewing and have a life-long interest in it.

Quilt 137
This view of Meta Snell's quilt was chosen by the team to be used on our information fliers right from the start of the project. It was felt appropriate as Weymouth had just been chosen as the venue for the sailing events and here we had boats and the seaside.

Quilt 192
"Welcome to England". Some of the most well known icons of England are portrayed from the flora and fauna to the British weather and our red post boxes.

Quilt 140
An Exmoor View. Exmoor is the smallest National Park in England and the quilt made by six friends is a reflection of this beautiful and quite isolated part of Britain. The land of Exmoor can be quite steep and has many valleys and rivers. It is best suited for grazing and especially for sheep.

Quilt 201
The seaside at Bournemouth is just so typically part of life in Britain. Sea and sand, beach huts and candy floss, searching for seashells and watching the boats are what we all do on our day by the sea.

Quilt 146
As Sheffield can boast several Sports Academies the Totley Brook Quilters each chose a sport to depict on their block for this quilt.

Quilt 225
Lincoln is the second largest, but one of the least well known counties of England, we are proud to celebrate just a few of the famous lives and heritage originating from our county.

Quilt 149
The quilt by Rowington Quilters "Green and Pleasant Land" depicts some of our diverse and beautiful island as though you are looking at it through a leaded window.

Quilt 234
"Hands of Friendship" was made by 17 young quilters aged between 7 and 17 years. Each of them appliquéd an outline of their hand, which they decorated with a variety of hand and machine stitches.

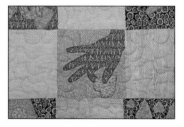

Quilt 177
The wide range of beautiful flowers of England have been recreated on this quilt as a lasting memory of a visit to this country.

Quilt 248
The county of Hampshire is shown by Albany Quilters in a variety of scenes from all around one of the most historic counties of England.

Quilt 280
An English village is shown on this quilt made by the Tunbridge Wells Quilters of Kent. All of village life is there to be seen by the visitors to our shores.

Quilt 355
Marigold Martin's quilt shows the silhouettes of the London skyline. A lasting memory for the athletes taking part in the London Games.

Quilt 363
This quilt was planned to represent the many churches that are found throughout Norfolk. There is an abundance of very early churches that have wonderful stained glass windows and brasses. This quilt gave the quilters the chance to be a little more experimental while still representing their area to the recipients. The central figure of the knight is based on an actual brass rubbing done by a member of the group.

Quilt 287
"My Home Town" by Dorothy Wheatley is a celebration of the City of Worcester. The river Severn, the swans and the ancient Cathedral are very much a part of the British heritage.

Quilt 269
Shakespeare's characters are captured by Elisabeth Green's beautiful embroidery together with some of the wonderful place names of Elizabethan England.

Quilt 416
Elisabeth Green's quilt "Star Line-up" is a celebration of the flowers of Great Britain brought to life by her beautiful embroidery.

Quilt 276
A small village nestles in the Hampshire countryside in this quilt called "This Green and Pleasant Land" by Christine Fell.

Quilt 450
Biggin Hill will forever be synonymous with the Battle of Britain. Now in much more peaceful times all the emblems of Kent are there to show the wide diversity of places and people of the county called "The Garden of England".

Quilt 350
"United in Sport". A very fitting title for a quilt showing icons for sports at the Olympics.

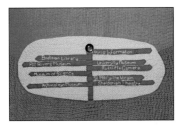

Quilt 473
The signpost fingers of this quilt show the places in Oxford that the visitors might sometimes miss. The maker wants us all to visit her town and see it as she sees it.

Be part of the UK's unique welcome to all the countries and athletes attending the 2012 Olympic Games and Paralympics in London.

You are invited to make and donate a quilt as a gift of friendship. It is intended that one quilt will be given to each country taking part in the Olympic Games and Paralympics.

inspired by London 2012

A GIFT OF QUILTS

Patron: Kaffe Fassett

www.agiftofquilts.co.uk   e-mail: agiftofquilts@yahoo.com

The Gallery of a Gift of Quilts

An A-Z of Countries

Kaffe Fassett & Brandon Mably starting the draw

Afghanistan

(No. 322) "Morris Dancing"
Anne Stacey
Olympic Games

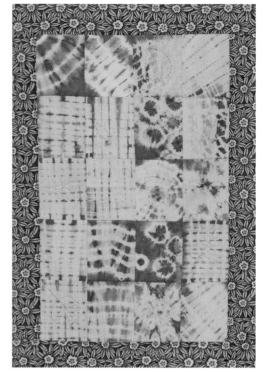

(No. 393) "Summer Flowers & Leaves"
Crondall Primary School
Paralympics

Albania

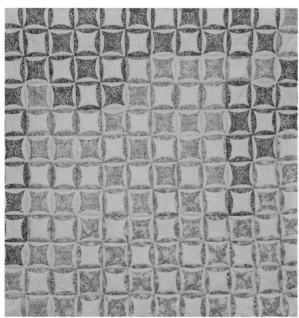

(No. 458) "Mosaics"
Sandy Tremlett
Olympic Games

(No. 74) "All Square"
Janette Francois
Paralympics

Algeria

(No. 106) "Rainbow Stars"
East Prawle Thursday Stitchers
Olympic Games

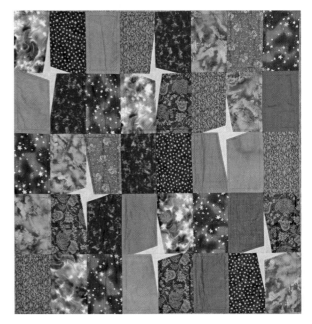

(No. 209) "Stargazer"
Gill Marshall
Paralympics

American Samoa

(No. 424) "Wild At Heart"
Janet Cull
Olympic Games

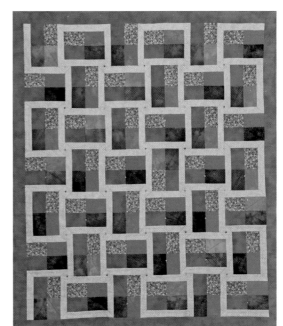

(No. 408) "Bright Mix"
Patsy Perrin
Paralympics

Andorra

(No. 495) "Round & Round"
Mary Jones
Olympic Games

(No. 278) "Carnival Time"
Jean Hayman
Paralympics

Angola

(No. 58) "London Icons (2)"
Hazel Allen
Olympic Games

(No. 155) "A Study In Blue and Yellow"
Baker Street Babes
Paralympics

Antigua & Barbuda

(No. 355) "Silhouettes in the City"
Marigold Martin
Olympic Games

(No. 263) "A Traditional Sampler"
Douglas Valley Quilters
Paralympics

Argentina

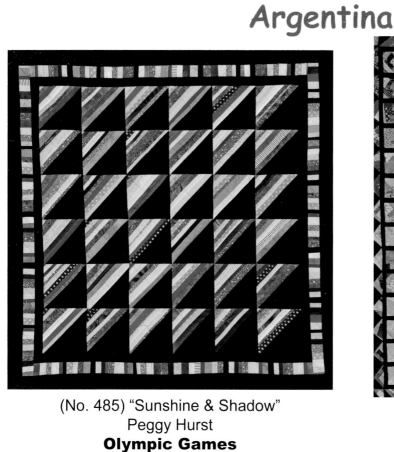

(No. 485) "Sunshine & Shadow"
Peggy Hurst
Olympic Games

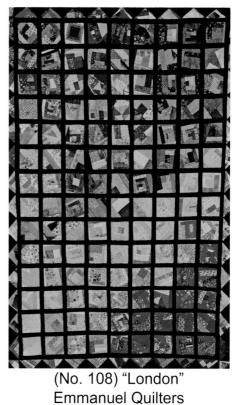

(No. 108) "London"
Emmanuel Quilters
Paralympics

Armenia

(No. 436) "Let's Celebrate Summer's Here"
Margaret Benting
Olympic Games

(No. 474) "Not My Colours"
Mandy Culling, quilted by Fir Tree Quilting
Paralympics

Aruba

(No. 90) "Dancing Around The World"
Ann Underhill
Olympic Games

Australia

(No. 248) "Where We Live"
Albany Quilt Group
Olympic Games

(No. 15) "Rainbows Shine On You"
Baker Street Babes
Paralympics

Austria

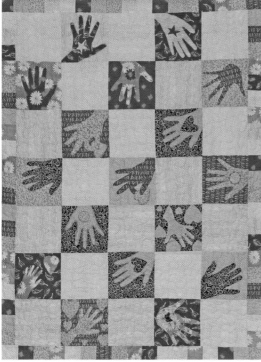

(No. 234) "Hands of Friendship"
Region 13A Young Quilters
Olympic Games

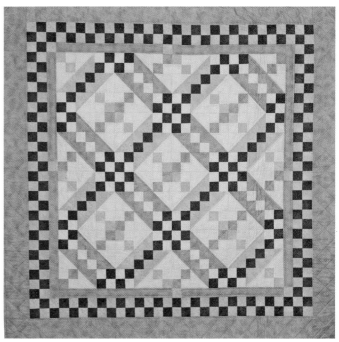

(No. 42) "Chequers"
Barbara Smith
Paralympics

Azerbaijan

(No. 87) "Wish upon a Star"
Elizabeth Ashley
Olympic Games

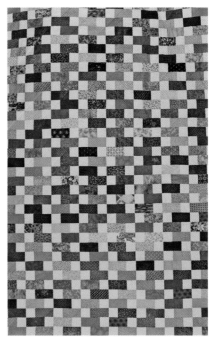

(No. 7) "The Blues"
Barbara Campbell
Paralympics

Bahamas

(No. 101) "Union Stars"
The Pumpkin Patchers
Olympic Games

Bahrain

(No. 399) "Many Stitches"
Kamaljit Chana (and sisters Harinda,
Manjit, Sharan, Sharan R & Veena)
Olympic Games

(No. 258) "On The Beach"
Anne Pearce
Paralympics

Bangladesh

(No. 45) "Autumn Golds"
Gladys Eves
Olympic Games

(No. 310) "Geometry"
Ingrid Mather
Paralympics

Barbados

(No. 324) "Swimming Lanes and Running Tracks"
Linda Cocksedge
Olympic Games

(No. 439) "From Sea To Sandy Shore"
Ann Cookson, finished by Elisabeth Green
Paralympics

Belarus

(No. 256) "Flags of Friendship"
Stitchmates
Olympic Games

(No. 440) "A Green And Pleasant Land"
Patricia Webb
Paralympics

Belgium

(No. 373) "Through The Square Window"
St Mary's Convent & Nursing Home
(Craft Group)
Olympic Games

(No. 185) "England - A Green And
Pleasant Land"
Ealing Charity Quilters
Paralympics

Belize

(No. 412) "Trip Around The World"
Carol Holland
Olympic Games

Benin

(No. 207) "Feathers From The Past"
Gwynfai Rees-Griffiths
Olympic Games

(No. 445) "Touching Stars"
Becky Sharp
Paralympics

Bermuda

(No. 64) "Sampler Blocks"
Pam Peffer
Olympic Games

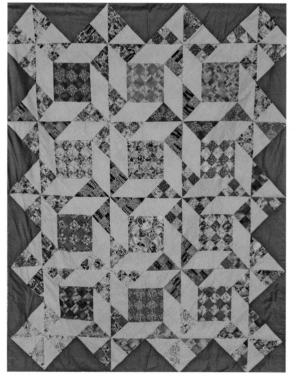

(No. 328) "Lemon Lime Fizz"
Jo-Anne Millington
Paralympics

Bhutan

(No. 88) "Stars Among The Flowers"
Barbara Westrop
Olympic Games

Bolivia

(No. 197) "For The Journey"
Pauline R Graves
Olympic Games

Bosnia & Herzegovina

(No. 488) "Crossing Borders"
Test Valley Quilters, quilted by Janie
Rowthorn
Olympic Games

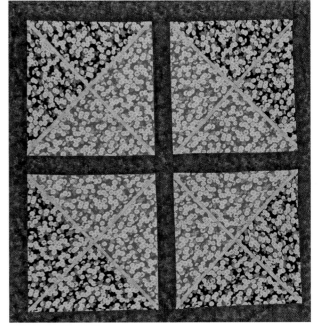

(No. 456) "Garden Of Friendship"
Soroptimist International of Kidderminster &
District Club
Paralympics

Botswana

(No. 377) "Caterwauling (in memory of
Marmaduke & Pickles)"
Patricia Pegg
Olympic Games

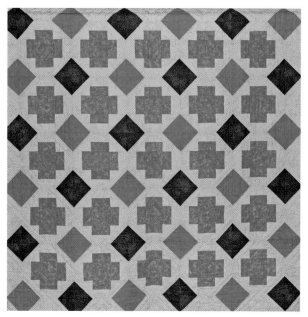

(No. 41) "Squares & Crosses"
Barbara Smith
Paralympics

Brazil

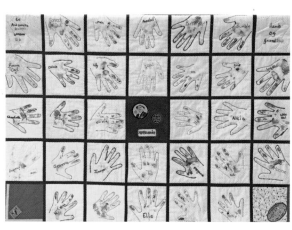

(No. 157) "Hands of Friendship"
1st Aldbourne Brownie Pack
Olympic Games

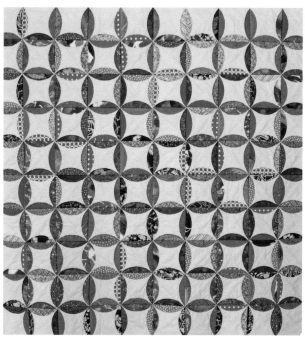

(No. 172) "Circle of Friends"
Mary Rawlins
Paralympics

British Virgin Islands

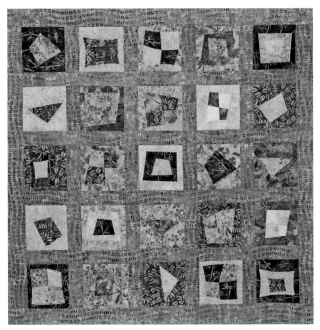

(No. 401) "Garden Reverie"
Andrea Murray
Olympic Games

Brunei

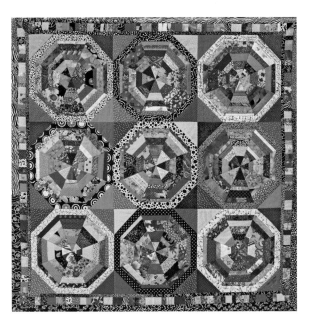

(No. 370) "All Around The World"
Ann Stamp
Olympic Games

(No. 190) "Podium Steps"
Test Valley Quilters, quilted by Sheila Wilkinson
Paralympics

Bulgaria

(No. 55) "Boat Medallion"
Hazel Allen
Olympic Games

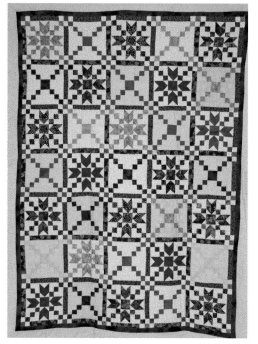

(No. 443) "Stepping Stones to Stardom"
Christina Gale
Paralympics

Burkina Faso

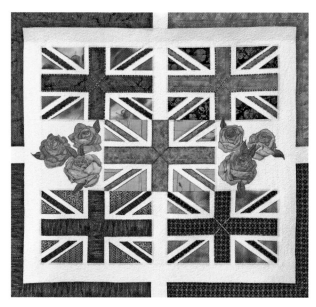

(No. 229) "Flags & Roses"
Patricia Collinson
Olympic Games

(No. 48) "Sunflowers"
Hazel Allen
Paralympics

Burundi

(No. 121) "Strawberries & Cream"
Mary Beesley
Olympic Games

(No. 186) "Red Square 2"
Ealing Charity Quilters
Paralympics

Cambodia

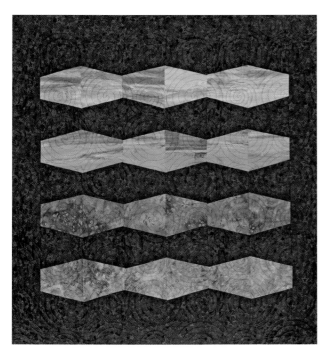

(No. 105) "Sea of Tranquility"
Ani Catt
Olympic Games

(No. 103) "Londinium MMXII"
Tillingbourne Valley Stitchers
Paralympics

Cameroon

(No. 496) "Can You Find The Cats"
Hazel Russell
Olympic Games

(No. 24) "Irish Jig"
Pauline Jones
Paralympics

Canada

(No. 2) "Kaleidoscope"
Helen Elgar
Olympic Games

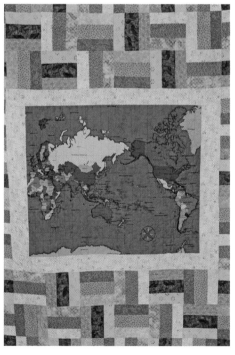

(No. 115) "Guiding Around The World"
1st West Horndean Rainbows, Brownies & Guides
Paralympics

Cape Verde

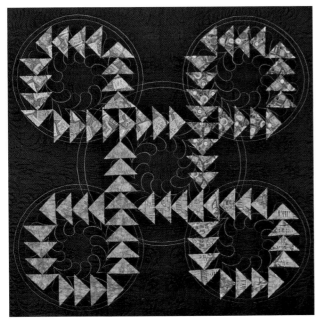

(No. 4) "Circles Around The World"
Test Valley Quilters, quilted by Izzy Hall
Olympic Games

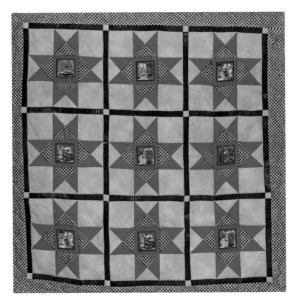

(No. 59) "London Icons (3)"
Hazel Allen
Paralympics

Cayman Islands

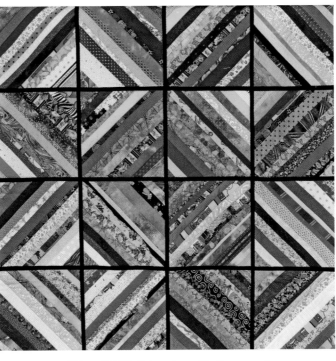

(No. 317) "Varying Pathways"
Ann Young
Olympic Games

Central African Republic

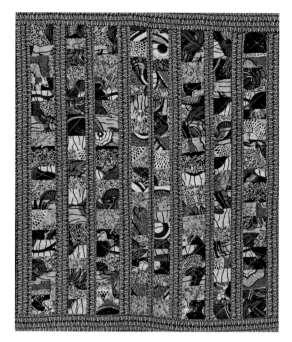

(No. 208) "Batik in Lines"
Joelynn Roberts
Olympic Games

(No. 303) "Good Luck"
Gail M. Walker
Paralympics

Chad

(No. 417) "Wedding Ring"
Brenda Bonner, quilted by Running Chicken
Olympic Games

Chile

(No. 350) "United in Sport"
Alvine Walker
Olympic Games

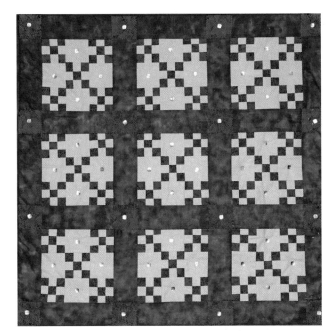

(No. 330) "Persevere"
Jean Marshall
Paralympics

China

(No. 477) "Halloween"
Doreen Hallet and Val Thomas
Olympic Games

(No. 62) "Iconic London"
Elizabeth Janes and Stephanie Allingham
Paralympics

Chinese Taipei

(No. 354) "Flying High"
Owl Quilters
Olympic Games

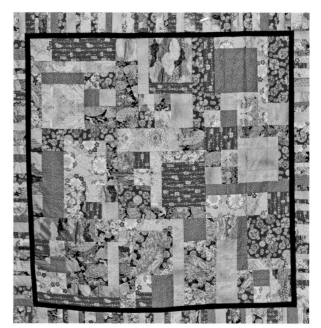

(No. 29) "Oriental Garden"
Margaret Moore
Paralympics

Columbia

(No. 162) "Sundazzle"
Julie Humphreys
Olympic Games

(No. 166) "False Start"
Veronica England
Paralympics

Comoros

Congo

(No. 433) "Around The Square"
Meta Snell
Olympic Games

(No. 287) "My Home Town"
Dorothy Wheatley and Elisabeth Green
Olympic Games

Cook Islands

(No. 446) "Sporting Colours"
Joan Hodgson
Olympic Games

Costa Rica

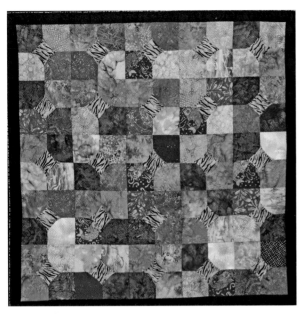

(No. 435) "Tiger's Eye"
Hartford Quilters
Olympic Games

(No. 346) "Perseverence"
Carol Moore and Eileen Hall
Paralympics

Cote-D'Ivoire

(No. 280) "The Village"
Tunbridge Wells Quilters
Olympic Games

(No. 434) "Well Spotted"
Claire Judd
Paralympics

Croatia

(No. 499) "Shades of Klee"
Test Valley Quilters, quilted by The Cotton Patch
Olympic Games

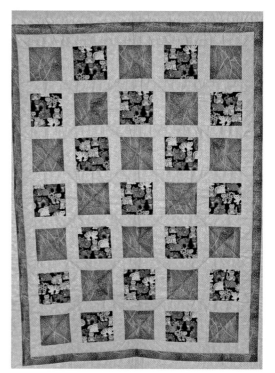

(No. 421) "Purrfect Cats"
Janet Turner and Carol Barton
Paralympics

Cuba

(No. 201) "Pleasures of Bournemouth"
Mary Short, quilted by Mandy Parks
Olympic Games

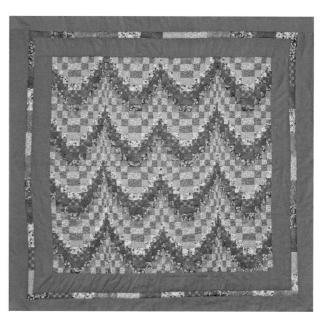

(No. 301) "Step Together"
Gillian Copperwheat
Paralympics

Cyprus

(No. 279) "Black & White and Red All Over"
Sue Goodridge, quilted by Fir Tree Quilting
Olympic Games

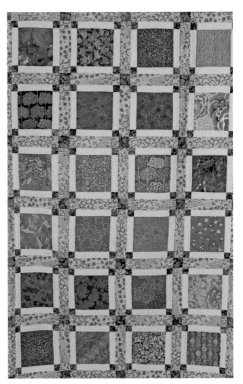

(No. 335) "Kernow Inspiration"
Pamela McLeod
Paralympics

Czech Republic

(No. 173) "Colours of Wessex"
Test Valley Quilters, quilted by Compton
Quilting Services
Olympic Games

(No. 236) "Stained Glass Magic"
Gillian Garner
Paralympics

Democratic Republic Of The Congo

(No. 486) "Best Year Of Your Life"
Lesley Gillespie
Olympic Games

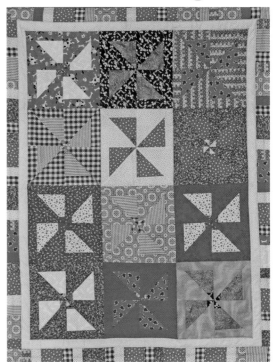

(No. 349) "Patriotic Pinwheels"
Aline Sheffield
Paralympics

Denmark

(No. 118) "Welsh Treasures"
Lucy Durston-Birt
Olympic Games

(No. 455) "All Square"
Elisabeth Green
Paralympics

Djibouti

(No. 345) "Lightning Stars"
Elizabeth Stuart
Olympic Games

(No. 79) "Formation Flying"
Hazel Wing
Paralympics

Dominica

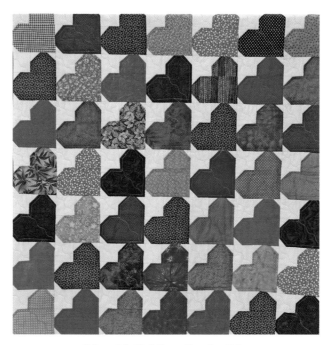

(No. 308) "Cardio Quilt"
Natalie Ings
Olympic Games

Dominican Republic

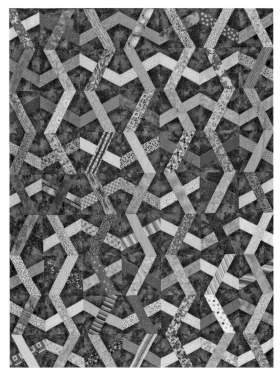

(No. 153) "Weaving Friendships"
Patchwork Friends
Olympic Games

(No. 54) "London Icons"
Hazel Allen
Paralympics

East Timor

(No. 454) "The Colours Of Scotland"
Joanne McCue
Olympic Games

(No. 304) "Pinwheel Quilt"
Lynn Brown
Paralympics

Ecuador

(No. 269) "A Touch Of Shakespeare"
Elisabeth Green
Olympic Games

(No. 344) "Flaming Stars"
Julia Sillitoe
Paralympics

Egypt

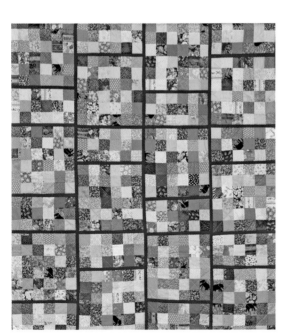

(No. 165) "Bright Delight"
Nythe Patchwork & Quilting Group
Paralympics

(No. 482) "First Off The Blocks"
Gail Phillips
Olympic Games

El Salvador

(No. 110) "All Stars"
Dorn Quilters,
Paralympics

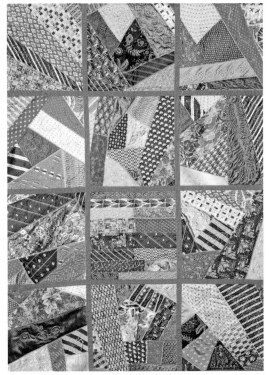

(No. 421) "Crazy Collection Of Gentlemen's Ties"
Peter Simpson
Olympic Games

Equatorial Guinea

(No. 274) "Around Womborne in 2011"
Wombourne Quilters
Olympic Games

Eritrea

(No. 205) "Check Mate"
Judy Fairless, quilted by Duxhurst Quilting
Olympic Games

Estonia

(No. 98) "Team Effort"
Uxbridge High School with Elisabeth Green
Paralympics

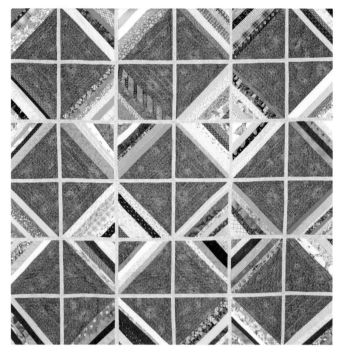

(No. 152) "Times Five"
Ardecca Group
Olympic Games

Ethiopia

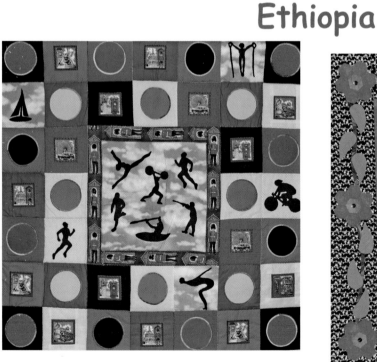

(No. 61) "Icons Circling London"
Elizabeth Janes, Debbie McKewon,
Stephanie Allingham
Olympic Games

(No. 314) "Black & White with a Splash of Red"
Catriona Burvill
Paralympics

Faroe Islands

(No. 140) "An Exmoor View"
Caroline Murtagh
Paralympics

Fiji

(No. 468) "Fan-antics for theOlympics"
Julie Humphreys
Olympic Games

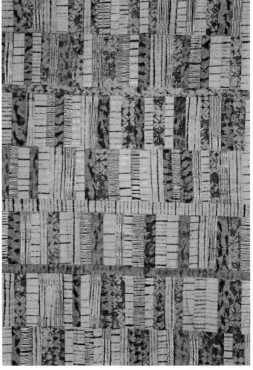

(No. 353) "Genome"
Maura Bangs
Paralympics

Finland

(No. 467) "Serendipity"
The Nuneaton Crop
Olympic Games

(No. 225) "Lincolnshire"
P & Q's Lincoln
Paralympics

France

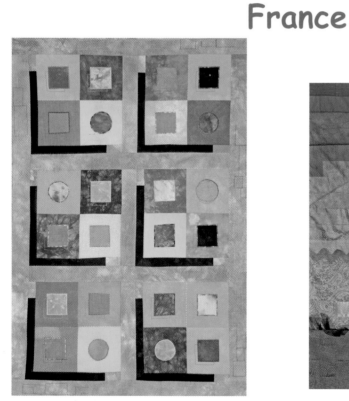

(No. 402) "Floating Squares"
Jeanette Huntley
Olympic Games

(No. 141) "View From My Window"
Jane Bull
Paralympics

Gabon

(No. 420) "Garden of England"
Joy Smith and Joyce Lewns
Olympic Games

(No. 441) "London Calling"
Patricia Webb
Paralympics

Georgia

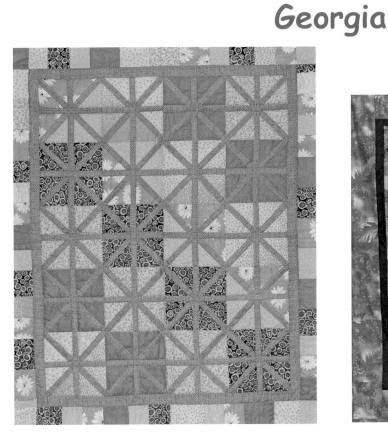

(No. 500) "The Many Colours of Coats"
Sharon Garrick
Olympic Games

(No. 375) "Coral Reef"
Joan Hinnes
Paralympics

Germany

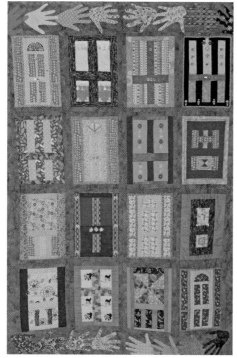

(No. 437) "Hands and Home"
East Malling Craft & Chat Group
Olympic Games

(No. 169) "Fanfare to the World"
Lunedale Quilters
Paralympics

Ghana

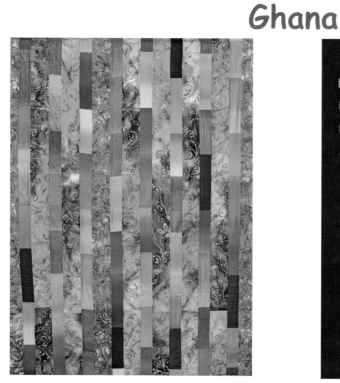

(No. 47) "All Batiks"
Gladys Eves
Olympic Games

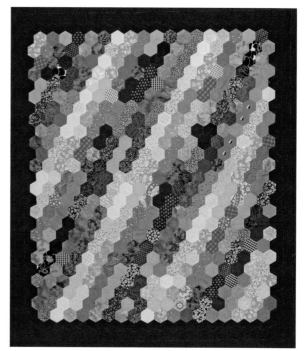

(No. 471) "The Rainbow"
Elizabeth Black and Judith Lovelady
Paralympics

Great Britain

(No. 11) "World Flags"
Charismatic Quilters
Olympic Games

(No. 286) "Welcome"
Elisabeth Green
Paralympics

Greece

(No. 216) "London Roads"
Jacqui Bradburn
Olympic Games

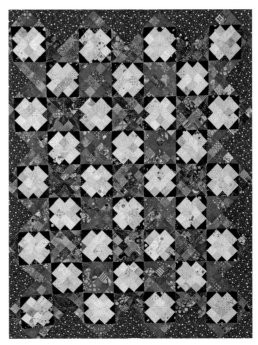

(No. 1991) "Everyone's A Star"
Valerie Arthur
Paralympics

Grenada

(No. 160) "London Green Spaces"
Carol Fletcher
Olympic Games

Guam

(No. 63) "Irish Cream"
Olga Donnelly
Olympic Games

(No. 257) "They're Playing Your Tune"
Anne Lloyd Williams
Paralympics

Guatemala

(No. 405) "Well Spotted"
Out of Africa, quilted by Hannah's Room
Olympic Games

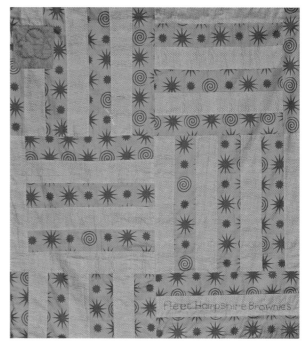

(No. 253) "Welcome From Fleet Brownies"
Fleet Brownies
Paralympics

Guinea

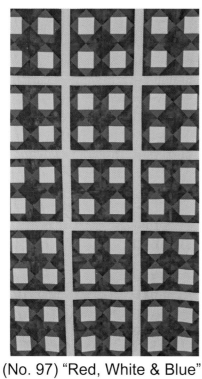

(No. 97) "Red, White & Blue"
BZB Quilters
Olympic Games

(No. 60) "Olympic Icons"
Elizabeth Janes
Paralympics

Guinea-Bissau

(No. 464) "English Garden"
Eve Young and Elisabeth Green
Olympic Games

Guyana

(No. 138) "By The Seaside"
West Wight Quilters
Paralympics

Haiti

(No. 8) "Peace and Liberty"
Tiddly Dyke Quilters, quilted by
Midsomer Quilting
Olympic Games

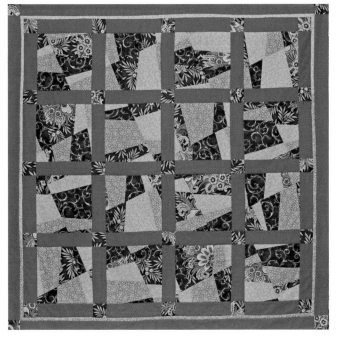

(No. 387) "Good Luck & Success"
Susan Tooze
Paralympics

Honduras

(No. 131) "Whitstable by the Sea"
Joy Smith and Joyce Lewns
Olympic Games

(No. 17) "Welcome Hearts and Flowers
Sampler Quilt"
Baker Street Babes
Paralympics

Hong Kong

(No. 67) "Crazy Triangles"
Eileen Maunder
Olympic Games

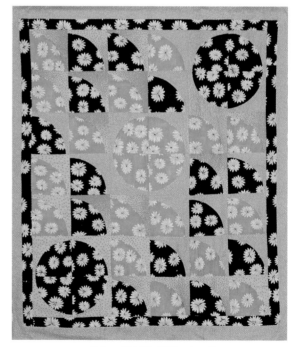

(No. 213) "Circles"
Joy Morgan
Paralympics

Iran

(No. 461) "Mabel's Dream"
Patricia Twigg
Olympic Games

(No. 203) "Flying High"
Havering Quilters
Paralympics

Iraq

(No. 18) "New England Sampler"
Baker Street Babes
Olympic Games

(No. 252) "Welcome from Fleet Rainbows"
Fleet Rainbows
Paralympics

Ireland

(No. 498) "Weymouth & Portland Wave to the World"
Test Valley Quilters, quilted by The Cotton Patch
Olympic Games

(No. 119) "Seasons"
Ladies of Crosspatch
Paralympics

Israel

(No. 414) "Flying High"
Christine Dobson
Olympic Games

(No. 415) "Spinning Stars"
Jenny Chalmers
Paralympics

Italy

(No. 395) "Inspired by Liberty"
Suzanne Foster
Olympic Games

(No. 466) "High Summer"
Patricia McKillop, quilted by Hannah's Room
Paralympics

Jamaica

(No. 272) "Navigation"
Jan Cornford
Olympic Games

(No. 438) "Poole Fanfare"
Ann Cookson, quilted by The Cotton Patch
Paralympics

Japan

(No. 416) "Star Line Up"
Elisabeth Green
Olympic Games

(No. 189) "Around The World with Sybil"
Test Valley Quilters, quilted by Fir
Tree Quilting
Paralympics

Jordan

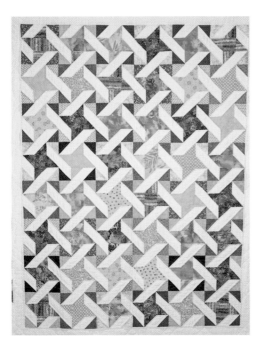

(No. 479) "Weaving Amongst The Stars"
Pat Simpson
Olympic Games

(No. 20) "Here's To You!"
Carol Mowat
Paralympics

Kazakhstan

(No. 113) "Running Wild LDN"
Linda Wild
Olympic Games

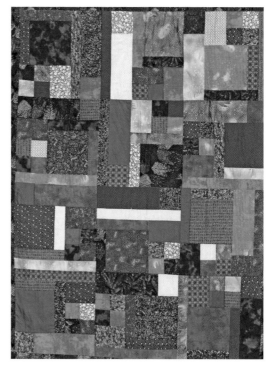

(No. 351) "Crossing The Line"
Jan Sowells, quilted by Helen Elgar
Paralympics

Kenya

(No. 126) "Something for Everyone"
Basingstoke & Old Basing U3A
Olympic Games

(No. 163) "Pinwheels"
Margaret Roberts
Paralympics

Kiribati

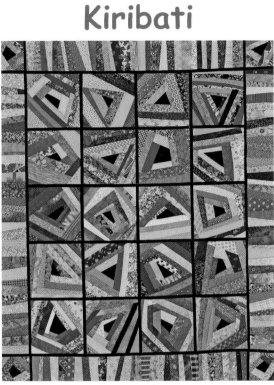

(No. 139) "Everybody's Colours"
King Alfred Quilters
Olympic Games

Kuwait

(No. 112) "Sussex by the Sea"
Seaford Day Group of the Ouse Valley Quilters
Olympic Games

(No. 202) "Friendship Braid"
Jean Edwards
Paralympics

Kyrgyzstan

(No. 270) "Brockley Star"
Brockley Quilters
Olympic Games

(No. 429) "Surrounded By Sea"
Sally Tritton
Paralympics

Laos

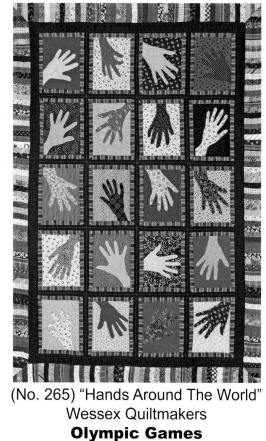

(No. 265) "Hands Around The World"
Wessex Quiltmakers
Olympic Games

(No. 218) "Blooming For Success"
Mary Parry
Paralympics

Latvia

(No. 491) "Scenes In Kent, the
Garden of England"
Olwen Coleman
Olympic Games

(No. 109) "Now You See Them,
Now You Don't"
Clifton Quilters
Paralympics

Lebanon

(No. 484) "All Buttoned Up"
Testwood Quilters
Olympic Games

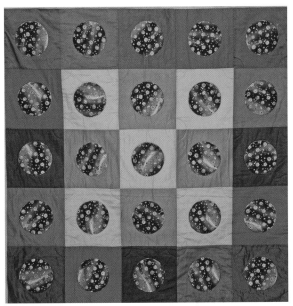

(No. 182) "Circles Allowed"
Elaine Langer
Paralympics

Lesotho

(No. 136) "Stars In Tilting Squares"
Meta Snell
Olympic Games

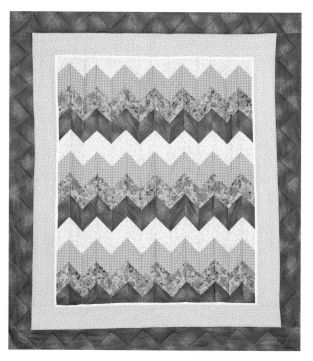

(No. 71) "Through An Autumn Forest"
Joy Carroll
Paralympics

Liberia

(No. 191) "Star Quality - Team Spirit"
Vivien Finch
Olympic Games

(No. 164) "Down Our Way"
Nythe Patchwork & Quilting Group
Paralympics

Libya

(No. 13) "Fantastic"
Jenny Keehan, quilted by TeePee Quilts
Olympic Games

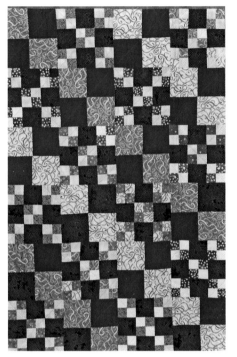

(No. 34) "Celebrations"
Gladys Eves
Paralympics

Liechtenstein

(No. 231) "Jazzy Stroud"
U3A Stroud
Olympic Games

(No. 233) "British Butterflies"
The London and Middlesex Region of the
Quilters Guild
Paralympics

Mauritius

(No. 33) "Red & Blue Stars"
Gladys Eves
Olympic Games

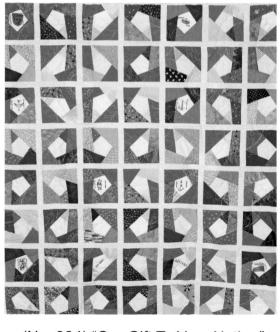

(No. 150) "In The Pink"
Angela Crook
Paralympics

Mexico

(No. 5) "Indigo Blues"
Pat Simmonds, quilted by Yvette Ness
Olympic Games

(No. 384) "Our Gift To Your Nation"
East Sussex Quilters
Paralympics

Micronesia

(No. 25) "Well Dressing"
Oakwood Quilters
Olympic Games

Moldova

(No. 53) "Anchor Medallion"
Hazel Allen
Olympic Games

(No. 249) "Clearing The Obstacles"
Brenda Ford
Paralympics

Monaco

(No. 305) "Aspiration"
Sue Collins
Olympic Games

Mongolia

(No. 295) "Twisted Mosaic"
Christine Porter
Olympic Games

(No. 276) "This Green and Pleasant Land"
Christine Fell
Paralympics

Montenegro

(No. 267) "Shining Through"
Maureen Hearn
Olympic Games

(No. 3) "Oriental Pizzazz"
Jenny Rundle, quilted by Mandy Parks
Paralympics

Morocco

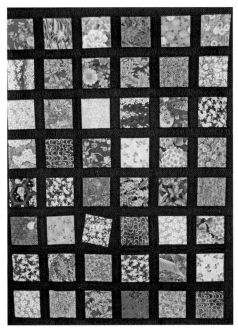

(No. 449) "Just In Time"
Virginia Cox
Olympic Games

(No. 425) "Cluster Of Stars"
Joan Frake
Paralympics

Mozambique

(No. 232) "Rhapsody In Blue"
The Quirky Quilters Burscough & District U3A
Olympic Games

(No. 102) "Stars United"
Sue Watters
Paralympics

Myanmar

(No. 96) "Pzazz"
Crazy Ladies of Surrey
Olympic Games

(No. 453) "The Colours of Scotland"
Muriel Campbell
Paralympics

Namibia

(No. 171) "The Green Hills of Home"
June Whitney
Olympic Games

Dreams take flight...

(No. 404) "Dreams Take Flight"
Diane Cowell
Paralympics

Nauru

(No. 369) "Colours of Scotland"
Kay Brooke
Olympic Games

Nepal

(No. 419) "Have A Go"
Women's Have A Go Group
Olympic Games

(No. 142) "Twelve Stars"
Jeny MacPhee
Paralympics

New Zealand

(No. 40) "Every Colour In Circles"
Gladys Eves
Olympic Games

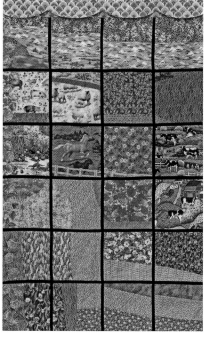

(No. 149) "Green & Pleasant Land"
Rowington Quilters
Paralympics

Nicaragua

(No. 457) "Mony a Mickle maks a Muckle"
Sew 'n' Sews
Olympic Games

Niger

(No. 31) "The Geese Fly Home"
Jan Urry
Olympic Games

(No. 174) "Go For Gold"
Elisabeth Green
Paralympics

Nigeria

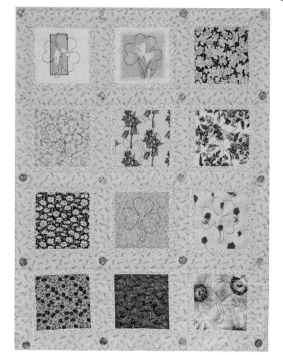

(No. 319) "The Natives"
LANZ
Olympic Games

(No. 124) "Crossing The Border"
Janet Sommerville
Paralympics

North Korea

(No. 311) "Geometry"
Hilary Sherratt
Olympic Games

Norway

(No. 251) "What a Mystery"
Jennifer Hills
Olympic Games

(No. 266) "Hands Of Friendship"
Wessex Quiltmakers
Paralympics

Oman

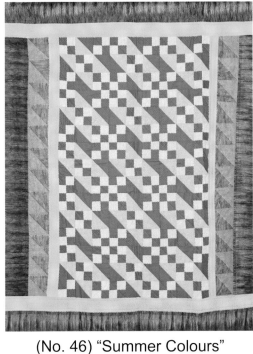

(No. 46) "Summer Colours"
Gladys Eves
Olympic Games

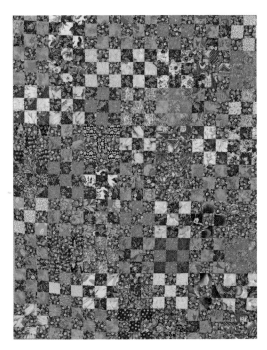

(No. 297) "An English Garden"
Ealing Charity Quilters
Paralympics

Papua New Guinea

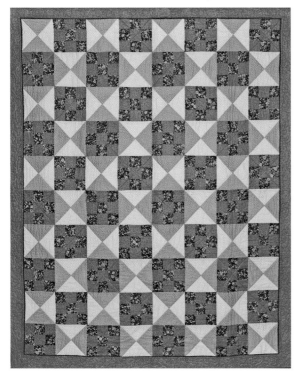

(No. 65) "Nine Patch & Triangles"
Pam Peffer
Olympic Games

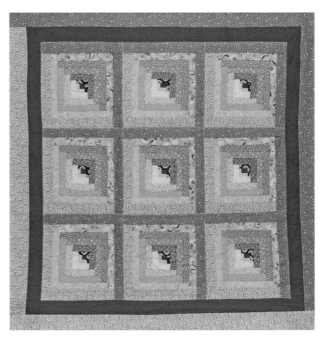

(No. 250) "Spring"
Rosemary Tremlett
Paralympics

Paraguay

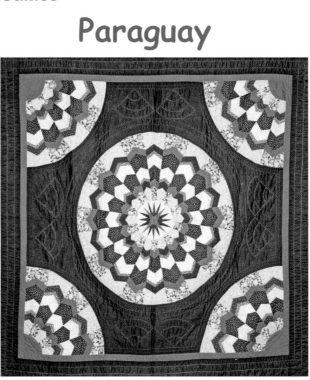

(No. 476) "A Different Sphinx"
Doreen Hallett
Olympic Games

Peru

(No. 57) "Ice Hockey"
Hazel Allen
Olympic Games

(No. 73) "Starting Point"
Gill Skinner
Paralympics

Poland

(No. 341) "Colours Of Summer"
Yvonne Blatchford
Olympic Games

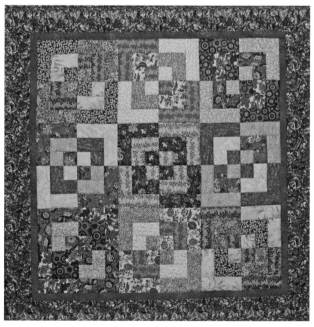

(No. 388) "Hopes, Dreams &
Successful Teams"
Michelle Tooze
Paralympics

Portugal

(No. 161) "Patriotic Pinwheels"
Quilters of All Saints Village
Olympic Games

(No. 51) "All Blue"
Hazel Allen
Paralympics

Puerto Rico

(No. 120) "Norfolk, UK"
Poringland Library Quilters
Olympic Games

(No. 137) "Land and Sea"
Meta Snell
Paralympics

Qatar

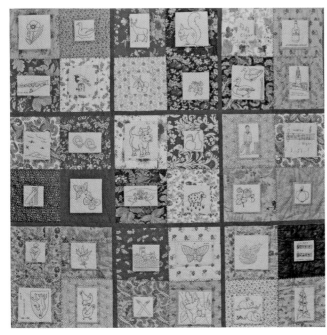

(No. 26) "Wonderful Worcestershire"
Springbank Quilters
Olympic Games

(No. 117) "Long Life & Harmony"
Margaret Wooller
Paralympics

Romania

(No. 406) "Country Garden"
Cranleigh Quilters
Olympic Games

(No. 148) "The Narrative Poem"
Jenny Hornsey
Paralympics

Russia

(No. 21) "Orbit"
Khurshid Bamboat
Olympic Games

(No. 128) "Amy's Coat"
Coats Crafts UK, quilted by Janie Rowthorn
Paralympics

Rwanda

(No. 334) "Memories of Malawi"
Sue Godfrey
Olympic Games

(No. 352) "Patriotic Pathways"
Rosemary McDonald, quilted by
Tiddly Dyke Quilters
Paralympics

Samoa

(No. 246) "Scrap Happy"
Lexie Bray
Olympic Games

(No. 77) "Dreaming Of Roses"
Edith Morris
Paralympics

San Marino

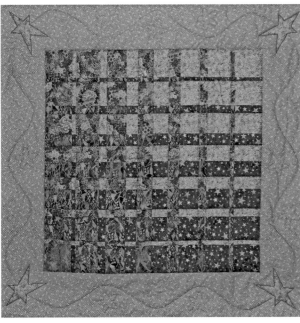

(No. 392) "Celebrations"
Kay Royce
Olympic Games

(No. 214) "Around the World in 80 days"
Freda Rawlins
Paralympics

Sao Tome & Principe

(No. 181) "Stars All Round"
Ann Spargo
Olympic Games

Saudi Arabia

(No. 358) "Flower Patch"
Cathy Clark
Olympic Games

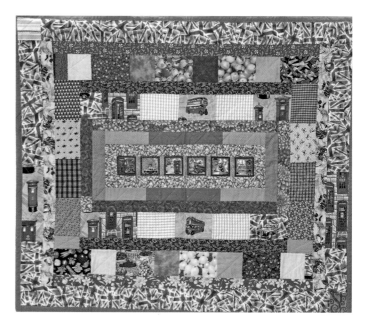

(No. 285) "Colourful London"
Wendy Cox
Paralympics

Senegal

(No. 389) "Diving In"
Sarah Payne
Olympic Games

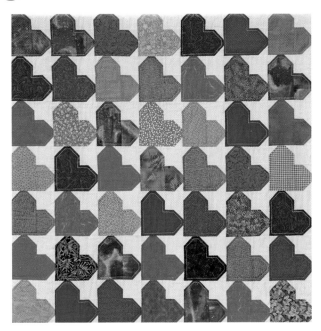

(No. 306) "Beating Hearts"
Di Richards
Paralympics

Serbia

(No. 86) "Sunflowers On The Green"
Elizabeth Ashley
Olympic Games

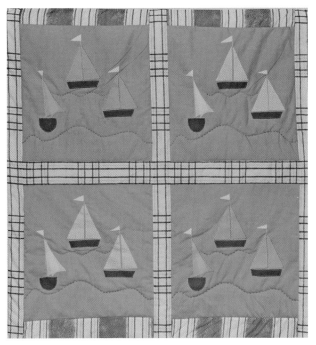

(No. 145) "Just Sailing"
Christine Doe
Paralympics

Seychelles

(No. 290) "Blue Windmills"
Eileen Postlethwaite
Olympic Games

Sierra Leone

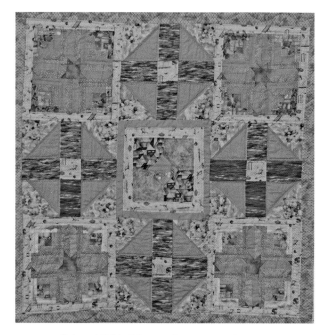

(No. 273) "Sun, Sea and Sand"
Michele Clarke
Olympic Games

(No. 196) "Up, Up and Away"
Hutton Priory Patchers
Paralympics

Singapore

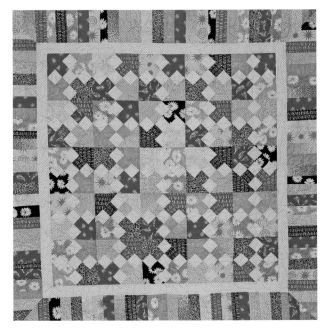

(No. 129) "On Target For Coats"
Coats Crafts UK, quilted by Kath Allaway
Olympic Games

(No. 151) "Jack In The Box"
Carol Reid
Paralympics

Slovakia

(No. 448) "A Medley For London"
Michelle Jolley
Olympic Games

(No. 365) "Bow Ties, Pearly Kings & Queens"
Pat Thomas
Paralympics

Slovenia

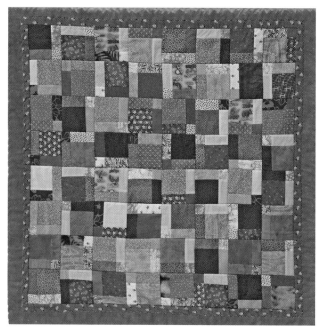

(No. 497) "Serendipity"
Muckhart Quilters
Olympic Games

(No. 298) "London Squares"
Ealing Charity Quilters
Paralympics

Solomon Islands

(No. 230) "The Playing Fields"
Christine Anderson
Olympic Games

Somalia

(No. 379) "Podium Quilt"
Eme Dean-Lewis
Olympic Games

A Gift Of Quilts

South Africa

(No. 450) "Biggin Hill"
Biggin Hill Stitchers
Olympic Games

(No. 89) "Tesselations"
Morag Bradshaw
Paralympics

South Korea

(No. 198) "Scraps of Red & Gold Dust"
Debbie Woolley
Olympic Games

(No. 178) "London Meets The World"
Test Valley Quilters, quilted by Kath Allaway
Paralympics

South Sudan

(No. 37) "Rosy Apples"
Gladys Eves
Olympic Games

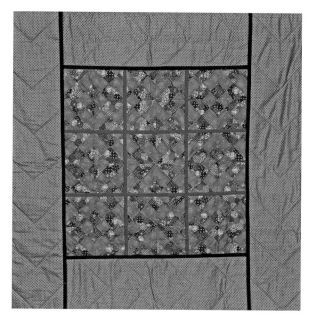

(No. 407) "Unity"
Bowerhill Busy Bees
Paralympics

Spain

(No. 156) "Hope For The Future"
Bob Anderton
Olympic Games

(No. 283) "Mardigras Windmills"
Mardigras Quilters, finished by
Elisabeth Green
Paralympics

Sri Lanka

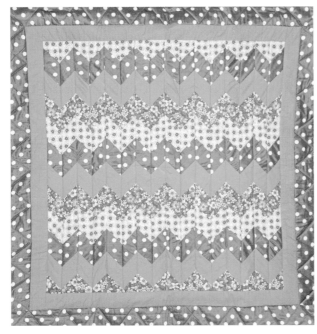

(No. 481) "Spaced Out On Spots"
Gail Phillips
Olympic Games

(No. 179) "Star Turn"
Marilyn Lovett
Paralympics

St Kitts & Nevis

(No. 459) "Patriotic Colours"
Anne Harris
Olympic Games

St Lucia

St Vincent & The Grenadines

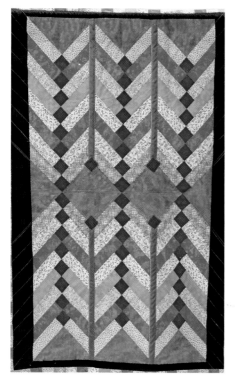

(No. 130) "Fantasy Flowers"
Hazel Russell
Olympic Games

(No. 259) "Lend A Hand"
1st Swanmore Brownies
Olympic Games

Sudan

(No. 409) "Fun in the Sun"
Mandy Downes
Olympic Games

(No. 210) "Fences to clear...Races to run..."
Margaret Harding
Paralympics

Suriname

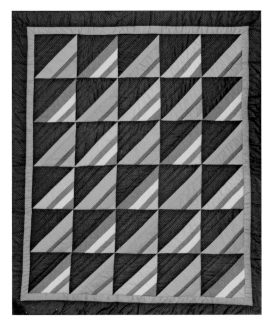

(No. 10) "Colours on Track"
Jenny Rundle
Olympic Games

(No. 340) "Wind in your Sails"
Windmill Quilters
Paralympics

Swaziland

(No. 81) "Photo Shoot"
Jean Jarvis
Olympic Games

Sweden

(No. 6) "In Transit"
Jenny Rundle, quilted by Jasmine Blackman
Olympic Games

(No. 348) "Cottage Garden"
Jane Wycherley
Paralympics

Switzerland

(No. 184) "Opus Anglicus Rosarum (English
Rose Work)"
Royal School of Needlework
Olympic Games

(No. 385) "Shades of Iris"
June Allen
Paralympics

Syria

(No. 85) "An English Country Garden"
Shirley Gibson
Olympic Games

(No. 195) "Messing About In Boats"
Margaret Johnson
Paralympics

Tajikistan

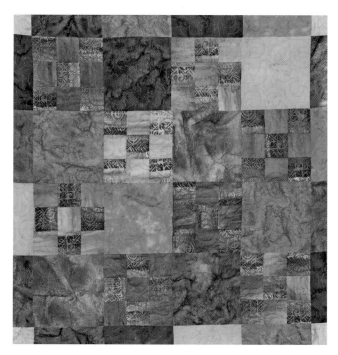

(No. 188) "Maori Dreams"
Angie Leary, quilted by Jude
Olympic Games

(No. 283) "Crazy Blocks"
Patricia Collinson
Paralympics

Tanzania

(No. 473) "This is my Oxford..."
Helle Gujral
Olympic Games

(No. 107) "A Quilt of Many Colours"
Shirley Quilters
Paralympics

Thailand

(No. 180) "Everyone had a go!"
Heswall Patchwork & Quilting Group
Olympic Games

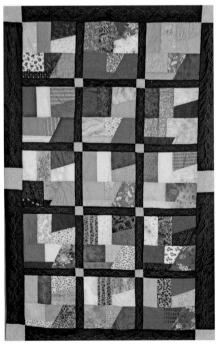

(No. 284) "Crazy For You"
Testwood Quilters
Paralympics

The Gambia

(No. 327) "Town and Country"
Gill Sharman
Olympic Games

The Netherlands

(No. 9) "Blue Iris"
Pat Simmonds and Jenny Rundle, quilted by
Mandy Parks
Olympic Games

(No. 23) "Ohio Stars"
Ruth Rodwell
Paralympics

The Phillippines

(No. 146) "Sporting Sheffield"
Totley Brook Quilters
Olympic Games

(No. 372) "Margaret's Quilt"
Margaret Gillmore
Paralympics

Timor-Leste

(No. 465) "Window on the Seasons"
Brockenhurst College Students
Olympic Games

(No. 223) "Pioneer Spirit"
Azalea Mayhew
Paralympics

Togo

(No. 307) "Memories of my Father P F DeBoerr"
Sue Smith
Olympic Games

Tonga

(No. 268) "Layers and Landmarks"
Pontypridd Women's Institute
Olympic Games

(No. 475) "Diamond Explosion"
Doreen Hallett
Paralympics

Trinidad & Tobago

(No. 239) "Multi-coloured Goose Chase"
Goose Chase Quilting, finished by
Elisabeth Green
Olympic Games

(No. 50) "Pretty Patches"
Hazel Allen
Paralympics

Tunisia

(No. 30) "Mary's Blockbender"
Mary Hewson
Olympic Games

(No. 242) "A World of Colours"
Gay Jenkins
Paralympics

Turkey

(No. 277) "Island of Dreams"
Waterside Quilters
Olympic Games

(No. 356) "Peace and Freedom"
Ingrid Osborn
Paralympics

Turkmenistan

(No. 76) "Pink Roses"
Edith Morris
Olympic Games

(No. 271) "Variations on Around the World"
Ringmer Quilters
Paralympics

Tuvalu

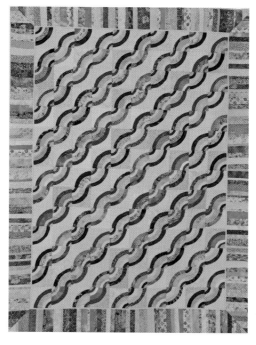

(No. 32) "Fractured Rainbows"
Barbara Hewett
Olympic Games

Uganda

(No. 83) "Winters' Night Sky"
Eileen Head
Olympic Games

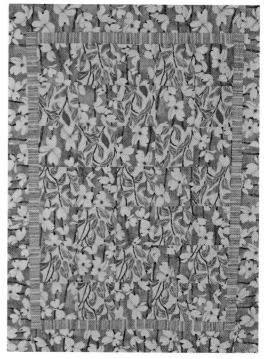

(No. 325) "Harmony"
Carole Sedgley & Butterfly Quilting
Paralympics

Ukraine

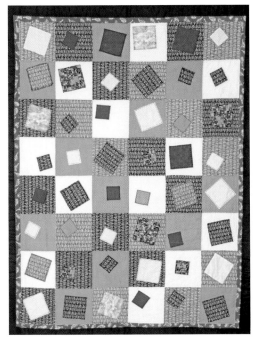

(No. 282) "Square Dance"
Michelle Clarke
Olympic Games

(No. 215) "An English Dawn"
Test Valley Quilters, quilted by
The Cotton Patch
Paralympics

United Arab Emirates

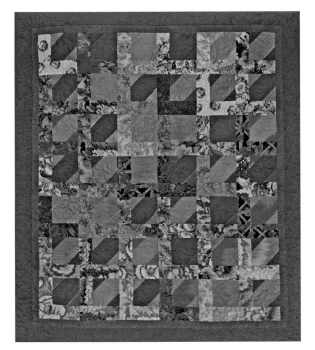

(No. 127) "Kaffe's Coat"
Coats Crafts UK, quilted by Mandy Parks
Olympic Games

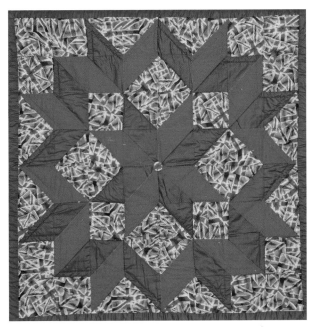

(No. 381) "Star Performance"
Caister Stitchers
Paralympics

United States of America

(No. 52) "Sampler"
Hazel Allen
Olympic Games

(No. 159) "Smoke at the Silk, Derby"
Julie Humphrey's
Paralympics

Uruguay

(No. 111) "Autumn Stars"
Wendy Curtis
Olympic Games

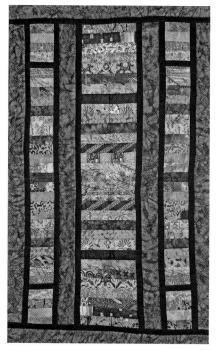

(No. 206) "Shopping at Maggie's"
Doris M Alcock
Paralympics

Uzbekistan

(No. 114) "Views of Norfolk"
Sewell Park Q & Ps
Olympic Games

(No. 187) "Jinny's Star"
Sarisberie Quilters
Paralympics

Vanuatu

(No. 451) "Chewton Mendip"
Chewton Mendip Women's Institute
Olympic Games

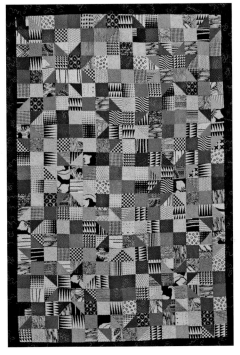

(No. 158) "Spirit of Global Harmony"
Liz Ferguson
Paralympics

Venezuela

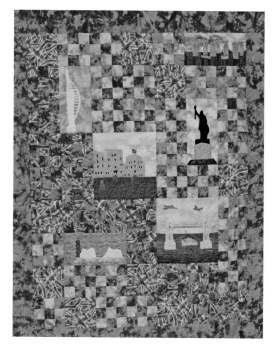

(No. 134) "Southern England"
Sue Butcher
Olympic Games

(No. 413) "Everyone's Dream"
Quilters Dream
Paralympics

Vietnam

(No. 427) "Seasons of England's
Lake District"
Levens Quilters
Olympic Games

(No. 411) "Hand of Friendship"
Jill Pentin
Paralympics

Virgin Islands

(No. 14) "Weather from England"
Baker Street Babes
Olympic Games

Yeman

(No. 23) "Made for You"
Juliet Simpson
Olympic Games

Zambia

(No. 487) "Tree of Life"
Test Valley Quilters, quilted by
Karen Cocksedge
Olympic Games

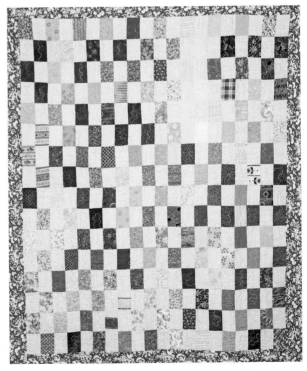

(No. 478) "Colourful Oblongs"
Pat Johnson
Paralympics

Zimbabwe

(No. 192) "Welcome to England"
Kennet Quilters
Olympic Games

(No. 38) "Stained Glass Flowers"
Gladys Eves
Paralympics

QUILTS FOR THE SPECIAL OLYMPICS

(No. 16) "Kate's Blue Stars"
Baker Street Babes
Special Olympics

(No. 19) "Hexagon Flower Garden"
Baker Street Babes
Special Olympics

(No. 35) "Blue Lagoon"
Gladys Eves
Special Olympics

(No. 36) "Flags Ahoy!"
Gladys Eves
Special Olympics

(No. 39) "Log Roll"
Gladys Eves
Special Olympics

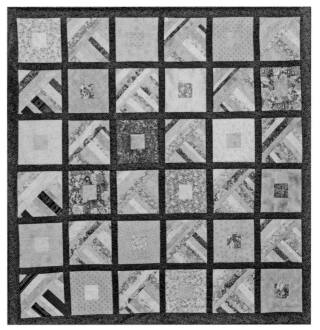

(No. 43) "Garden Flowers (1)"
E Ambrose
Special Olympics

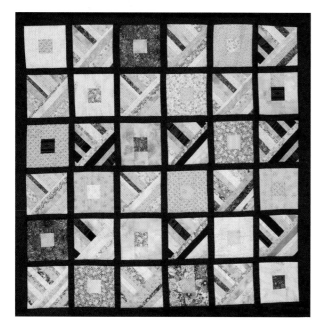

(No. 44) "Garden Flowers (2)"
E Ambrose
Special Olympics

(No. 56) "Horses for Courses"
Hazel Allen
Special Olympics

(No. 66) "Blue Garden"
Eileen Maunder
Special Olympics

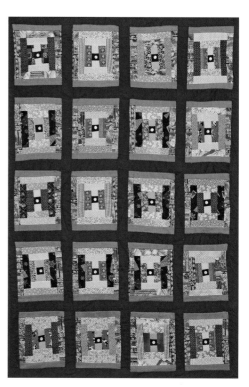

(No. 68) "Log Cabin"
Sheila Lane
Special Olympics

(No. 69) "Corner Stripes"
Sheila Rudling
Special Olympics

(No. 70) "Use The Blue Stepping
Stones Please"
Sheila Rudling
Special Olympics

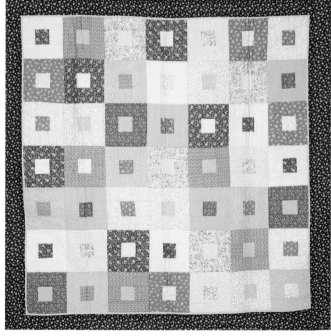

(No. 72) "Town Window Boxes"
Joy Carroll
Special Olympics

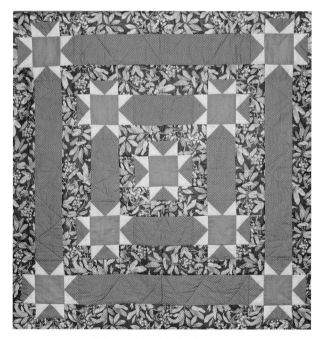

(No. 75) "Pink Stars"
Gail Phillips
Special Olympics

(No. 78) "Starting Blocks"
Chris Shergold
Special Olympics

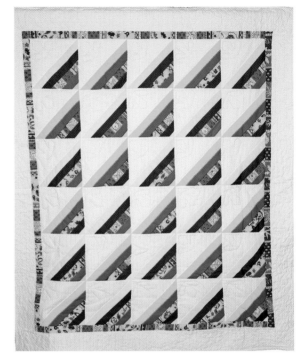

(No. 80) "Shading My Corner"
Sheila Rudling
Special Olympics

(No. 143) "Stormy Seas & Seashore"
Margaret Setchell
Special Olympics

(No. 144) "Devon Delights"
Kay Mannion
Special Olympics

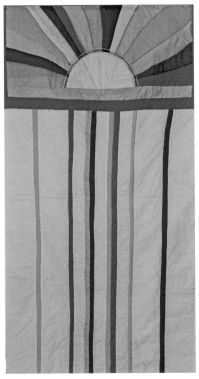

(No. 167) "Door to the Future"
Najlaa Khali
Special Olympics

(No. 170) "Wacky Trellis Quilt"
Baker Street Babes
Special Olympics

(No. 211) "Friendship Star from London"
Pinewood Quilters
Special Olympics

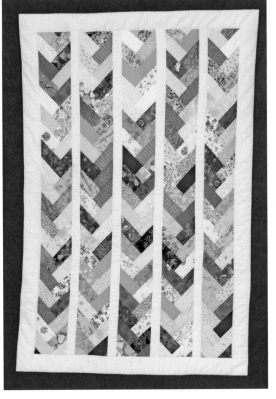

(No. 224) "Pioneer Pathways"
Sara Courtenay
Special Olympics

(No. 235) "In The Pink"
Christine Parker
Special Olympics

(No. 237) "Pink & Blue Shapes"
Gillian Garner, Vickie Fisher,
Kathryn Denton-Irwin
Special Olympics

(No. 238) "Roses"
Gillian Garner and Vickie Fisher
Special Olympics

(No. 241) "Mirror Image"
Shirley Payne
Special Olympics

A Gift Of Quilts

(No. 243) "Sunset in the Garden"
Tilly Bulling
Special Olympics

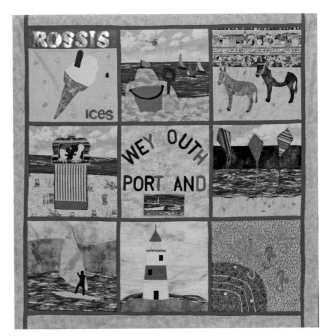

(No. 260) "Memories of Weymouth
& Portland"
Sandra Darvill
Special Olympics

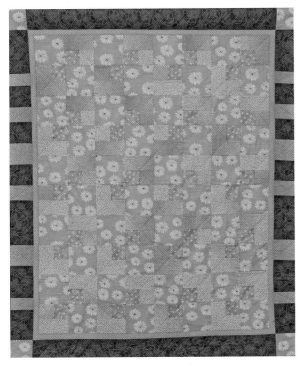

(No. 262) "Look on the Bright Side"
Jenny Cottier
Special Olympics

(No. 294) "Hearts"
Denise Stone
Special Olympics

(No. 331) "Bright Colours"
Mary Mason
Special Olympics

(No. 343) "Star Fish"
Antonella Jones
Special Olympics

(No. 366) "One Step at a Time"
Sharyn Hutchings
Special Olympics

(No. 367) "Ties of Friendship"
Julie Barbour
Special Olympics

A Gift Of Quilts

(No. 382) "Pride of London"
Penny Loaf Patchers
Special Olympics

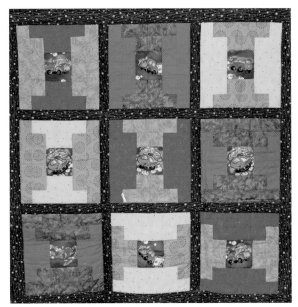

(No. 426) "Have a Ride"
Joan Frake
Special Olympics

(No. 447) "Boxes of Friendship"
MACK Patchwork Group
Special Olympics

(No. 452) "Going For Gold"
Maureen McCall
Special Olympics

(No. 462) "Spot The Red"
Phyllis Learoyd
Special Olympics

(No. 490) "The Devon Thatched Cottage"
Yvonne Johnson
Special Olympics

(No. 494) "Endeavour"
Valerie Hayes
Special Olympics

Alphabetical index by Quilt Maker

Key: Quilt presented to Olympics (O), Paralympics (P), Special Olympics (S)

A

1st Aldbourne Brownie Pack, *Hands of Friendship*, Brazil (O)

Albany Quilt Group, *Where We Live*, Australia (O)

Alcock, Doris M, *Shopping at Maggie's*, Uruguay (P)

Allen, Hazel,
All Blue, Portugal (P)
Anchor Medallion, Moldova (O)
Boat Medallion, Bulgaria (O)
Horses for Courses, (S)
Ice Hockey, Peru (O)
London Icons, Dominican Republic (P)
London Icons (2), Angola (O)
London Icons (3), Cape Verde (P)
Pretty Patches, Trinidad & Tobago (P)
Sampler, United States of America (O)
Ship Medallion, Malaysia (P)
Sunflowers, Burkina Faso (P)

Allen, June, *Shades of Iris*, Switzerland (P)

Ambrose, E,
Garden Flowers (1), (S)
Garden Flowers (2), (S)

Anderson, Christine, *The Playing Fields*, Solomon Islands (O)

Anderton, Bob, *Hope for the Future*, Spain (O)

Ardecca Group, *Times Five*, Estonia (O)

Arthur, Valerie, *Everyone's a Star*, Greece (P)

Ashley, Elizabeth,
Sunflowers on the Green, Serbia (O)
Wish upon a Star, Azerbaijan (O)

B

Baker Street Babes,
A Study in Blue & Yellow, Angola (P)
Hexagon Flower Garden, (S)
Hearts & Flowers Sampler Quilt, Honduras (P)
Kate's Blue Stars, (S)
New England Sampler, Iraq (O)
Rainbows Shine on You, Australia (P)
Wacky Trellis Quilt, (S)
Weather from England, Virgin Islands (O)

Bamboat, Khurshid, *Orbit*, Russia (O)

Bangs, Maura, *Genome*, Fiji (P)

Barbour, Julie, *Ties of Friendship*, (S)

Basingstoke and Old Basing U3A, *Something for Everyone*, Kenya (O)

Beesley, Mary, *Strawberries & Cream*, Burundi, (O)

Benting, Margaret, *Let's Celebrate Summer's Here*, Armenia (O)

Biggin Hill Stitchers, *Biggin Hill*, South Africa (O)

Black, Elizabeth & Judith Lovelady, *The Rainbow*, Ghana (P)

Blatchford, Yvonne, *Colours of Summer*, Poland (O)

Bonner, Brenda, quilted by Running Chicken, *Wedding Ring*, Chad (O)

Bowerhill Busy Bees, *Unity*, South Sudan (P)

Bradburn, Jacqui, *London Roads*, Greece (O)

Bradshaw, Morag, *Tesselations*, South Africa (P)

Bray, Lexie, *Scrap Happy*, Samoa (O)

Bridgman, Angela, *Land, Sea and Sky*, Mali (P)

Brockenhurst College Students, *Window on the Seasons*, Timor-Leste (O)

Brockley Quilters, *Brockley Star*, Kyrgyzstan (O)

Brooke, Kay, *Colours of Scotland*, Nauru (O)

Brown, Lynn, *Pinwheel Quilt*, East Timor (P)

Bull, Jane, *View from my Window*, France (P)

Bulling, Tilly, *Sunset in the Garden*, (S)

Burvill, Catriona, *Black & White with a Splash of Red*, Ethiopia (P)

Butcher, Sue, *Southern England*, Venezuela (O)

BZB Quilters, *Red, White & Blue*, Guinea (O)

C

Caister Stitchers, *Star Performance*, United Arab Emirates (P)

Campbell, Barbara, *The Blues*, Azerbaijan (P)

Campbell, Muriel, *The Colours of Scotland*, Myanmar (P)

Carroll, Joy,
Through an Autumn Forest, Lesotho (P)
Town Window Boxes, (S)

Catt, Ani, *Sea of Tranquility*, Cambodia (O)

Chace Community School, *Red, White & Black*, India (P)

Chalmers, Jenny, *Spinning Stars*, Israel (P)

Chana, Kamaljit and sisters, Harinder, Manjit, Sharan, Sharan R & Veena, *Many Stitches*, Bahrain (O)

Charismatic Quilters, *World Flags*, Great Britain (O)

Chewton Mendip Women's Institute, *Chewton Mendip*, Vanuatu (O)

Clark, Cathy, *Flower Patch*, Saudi Arabia (O)

Clark, Joy, *Red Communication*, India (O)

Clarke, Michele,
Square Dance, Ukraine (O)
Sun, Sea and Sand, Sierra Leone (O)

Clifton Quilters, *Now You See Them, Now You Don't!* Latvia (P)

Coats Crafts UK,
quilted by Janie Rowthorn, *Amy's Coat*, Russia (P)
quilted by Mandy Parks, *Kaffe's Coat*, United Arab Emirates (O)
quilted by Kath Allaway, *On Target for Coats*, Singapore (O)

Cocksedge, Linda, *Swimming Lanes & Running Tracks*, Barbados (O)

Cohen, Deborah, *We Can All Fit*, Macedonia (O)

Coleman, Olwen, *Scenes In Kent: The Garden of England*, Latvia (O)

Collins, Deborah, *Harmony*, Malaysia (O)

Collins, Sue, *Aspiration*, Monaco (O)

Collinson, Patricia,
Crazy Blocks, Tajikistan (P)
Flags & Roses, Burkina Faso (O)

Cookson, Ann,
finished by Elisabeth Green, *From Sea to Sandy Shore*, Barbados (P)
quilted by The Cotton Patch, *Poole Fanfare*, Jamaica (P)

Copperwheat, Gillian, *Step Together*, Cuba (P)

Cornford, Jan, *Navigation*, Jamaica (O)

Cottier, Jenny, *Look on the Bright Side*, (S)

Courtenay, Sara, *Pioneer Pathways*, (S)

Cowell, Diane, *Dreams Take Flight*, Namibia (P)

Cox, Virginia, *Just in Time*, Morocco (O)

Cox, Wendy, *Colourful London*, Saudi Arabia (P)

Cranleigh Quilters, *Country Garden*, Romania (O)

Crazy Ladies of Surrey, *Pzazz*, Myanmar (O)

Crondall Primary School, *Summer Flowers & Leaves*, Afghanistan (P)

Crook, Angela, *In the Pink*, Mauritius (P)

Cull, Janet, *Wild at Heart*, American Samoa (O)

Culling, Mandy, quilted by Fir Tree Quilting, *Not My Colours*, Armenia (P)

Curtis, Wendy, *Autumn Stars*, Uruguay (O)

D

Darvill, Sandra, *Memories of Weymouth & Portland*, (S)

Dean-Lewis, Eme, *Podium Quilt*, Somalia (O)

Dobson, Christine, *Flying High*, Israel (O)

Doe, Christine, *Just Sailing*, Serbia (O)

Dolding, Audrey, *Pinwheel Medley*, Hungary (P)

Donnelly, Olga, *Irish Cream*, Guam (O)

Dorn Quilters, *All Stars*, El Salvador (P)

Douglas Valley Quilters, *A Traditional Sampler*, Antigua & Barbuda (P)

Downes, Mandy, *Fun in the Sun*, Sudan (O)

Durston-Birt, Lucy, *Welsh Treasures*, Denmark (O)

E

Ealing Charity Quilters,
An English Garden, Oman (P)
England – A Green & Pleasant Land, Belgium (P)
London Squares, Slovenia (P)
Red Square 2, Burundi (P)

East Malling Craft & Chat Group, *Hands and Home*, Germany (O)

East Prawle Thursday Stitchers, *Rainbow Stars*, Algeria (O)

East Sussex Quilters, *Our Gift to Your Nation*, Mexico (P)

Edwards, Jean, *Friendship Braid*, Kuwait (P)
Elgar, Helen, *Kaleidoscope*, Canada (O)
Emmanuel Quilters, *London*, Argentina (P)
England, Veronica, *False Start*, Columbia (P)
Eves, Gladys,
    All Batiks, Ghana (O)
    Autumn Golds, Bangladesh (O)
    Blue Lagoon, (S)
    Celebrations, Libya (P)
    Every Colour in Circles, New Zealand (O)
    Flags Ahoy! (S)
    Log Roll, (S)
    Red & Blue Stars, Mauritius (O)
    Rosy Apples, South Sudan (O)
    Stained Glass Flowers, Zimbabwe (P)
    Summer Colours, Oman (O)

F
Fairless, Judy, quilted by Duxhurst Quilting, *Check Mate*, Eritrea (O)
Fell, Christine, *This Green & Pleasant Land,* Mongolia (P)
Ferguson, Liz, *Spirit of Global Harmony*, Vanuatu (P)
Finch, Vivien, *Star Quality – Team Spirit*, Liberia (O)
Fleet Brownies, *Welcome from Fleet Brownies*, Guatemala (P)
Fleet Rainbows, *Welcome from Fleet Rainbows*, Iraq (P)
Fletcher, Carol, *London's Green Spaces*, Grenada (O)
Ford, Brenda, *Clearing the Obstacles*, Moldova (P)
Foster, Suzanne, *Inspired by Liberty*, Italy (O)
Frake, Joan,
    Cluster of Stars, Morocco (P)
    Have a Ride, (S)
Francois, Janette, *All Square*, Albania (P)

G
Gale, Christina, *Stepping Stones to Stardom*, Bulgaria (P)
Galloway, Colette, *Mountain, What Mountain?* Luxembourg (P)
Garner, Gillian, *Stained Glass Magic*, Czechoslovakia Republic (P)
Garner, Gillian; Vickie Fisher & Kathryn Denton-Irwin, *Pink & Blue Shapes* (S)
Garner, Gillian & Vickie Fisher, *Roses* (S)
Garrick, Sharon, *The Many Colours of Coats*, Georgia (O)
Gibson, Shirley,
    An English Country Garden, Syria (O)
    Sunflowers at Sunset, Malta (P)
Gillespie, Lesley, *Best Year of Your Life*, Democratic Republic of the Congo (O)
Gillmore, Margaret, *Margaret's Quilt*, The Philippines (P)
Godfrey, Sue, *Memories of Malawi*, Rwanda (O)
Goodridge, Sue, quilted by Fir Tree Quilting, *Black & White and Red All Over*, Cyprus (O)
Goose Chase Quilting, finished by Elisabeth Green, *Multi-coloured Goose Chase*, Trinidad & Tobago (O)
Graves, Pauline R, *For the Journey*, Bolivia (O)
Green, Elisabeth,
    All Square, Denmark (P)
    A Touch of Shakespeare, Ecuador (O)
    Go for Gold, Niger (P)
    Star Line Up, Japan (O)
    The Winner's Bouquet, Indonesia (O)
    Welcome, Great Britain (P)

Gujral, Helle, *This is my Oxford…*, Tanzania (O)

H
Hallett, Doreen,
    A Different Sphinx, Paraguay (O)
    Diamond Explosion, Tonga (P)
Hallett, Doreen & Val Thomas, *Halloween*, China (O)
Halstead, Val, *Patriotic Colours*, Madagascar (O)
Harding, Margaret, *Fences to Clear… Races, to Run...*, Sudan (P)
Harris, Anne, *Patriotic Colours*, St Kitts & Nevis (O)
Hartford Quilters, *Tiger's Eye*, Costa Rica (O)
Havering Quilters, *Flying High*, Iran (P)
Hayes, Val, *Endeavour*, (S)
Hayman, Jean, *Carnival Time*, Andorra (P)
Head, Eileen,
    Monkey Business, Mauritania (P)
    Winters' Night Sky, Uganda (O)
Hearn, Maureen, *Shining Through*, Montenegro (O)
Heswall Patchwork & Quilting Group, *Everyone Had a Go!* Thailand (O)
Hewett, Barbara, *Fractured Rainbows*, Tuvalu (O)
Hewson, Mary, *Mary's Blockbender*, Tunisia (O)
Hickman, Judy, *Margaret's Mystery*, Iceland (P)
Hills, Jennifer, *What a Mystery*, Norway (O)
Hinnes, Joan, *Coral Reef*, Georgia (P)
Hodgson, Joan, *Sporting Colours*, Cook Islands (O)
Holland, Carol, *Trip Around the World*, Belize (O)
Hornsey, Jenny, *The Narrative Poem*, Romania (P)
Humphreys, Julie,
    Fan-antics for the Olympics, Fiji (O)
    Smoke at the Silk, Derby, United States of America (P)
    Sundazzle, Columbia (O)
Huntley, Jeanette, *Floating Squares*, France (O)
Hurst, Peggy, *Sunshine & Shadow*, Argentina (O)
Hutchings, Sharyn, *One Step at a Time*, (S)
Hutton Priory Patchers, *Up, Up and Away*, Sierra Leone (P)

I
Ings, Natalie, *Cardio Quilt*, Dominica (O)

J
Janes, Elizabeth, *Olympic Icons*, Guinea (P)
Janes, Elizabeth & Stephanie Allingham, *Iconic London*, China (P)
Janes, Elizabeth, Stephanie Allingham & Debbie McKewon, *Icons Circling London*, Ethiopia (O)
Jarvis, Jean, *Photo Shoot*, Swaziland (O)
Jenkins, Gay, *A World of Colours*, Tunisia (P)
John Clare School Helpston, *Helpston Red White & Blue*, Lithuania (O)
Johnson, Margaret, *Messing About in Boats*, Syria (P)
Johnson, Pat, *Colourful Oblongs*, Zambia (P)
Johnson, Yvonne, *The Devon Thatched Cottage*, (S)

Jolley, Michelle, *A Medley for London*, Slovakia (O)
Jones, Antonella, *Star Fish*, (S)
Jones, Mary, *Round & Round*, Andorra (O)
Jones, Pauline, *Irish Jig*, Cameroon (P)
Judd, Claire, *Well Spotted*, Cote-d'Ivoire (P)

K
Keehan, Jenny, quilted by TeePee Quilts, *Fantastic*, Libya (O)
Kennet Quilters, *Welcome to England*, Zimbabwe (O)
Khali, Najlaa, *Door to the Future*, (S)
King Alfred Quilters, *Everybodies Colours!* Kiribati (O)
Knight, Margaret, *Athletic Stars*, Macau (P)

L
Ladies of Crosspatch, *Seasons*, Ireland (P)
Lane, Sheila, *Log Cabin*, (S)
Langer, Elaine,
    Circles Allowed, Lebanon (P)
    Superstar – That's What You Are! Palestine (O)
LANZ – Libby, Audrey, Niki & Zandra, *The Natives*, Nigeria (O)
Leary, Angie, quilted by Jude, *Maori Dreams*, Tajikistan (O)
Learoyd, Phyllis, *Spot the Red*, (S)
Levens Quilters, *Seasons of England's Lake District*, Vietnam (O)
Lloyd Williams, Anne, *They're Playing Your Tune*, Guam (P)
Lovett, Marilyn, *Star Turn*, Sri Lanka (P)
Lunedale Quilters, *Fanfare to the World*, Germany (P)

M
MACK Patchwork Group, *Boxes of Friendship*, (S)
MacPhee, Jeny, *Twelve Stars*, Nepal (P)
Mannion, Kay, *Devon Delights*, (S)
Mardigras Quilters, finished by Elisabeth Green, *Mardigras Windmills*, Spain (P)
Marshall, Gill, *Stargazer*, Algeria (O)
Marshall, Jean, *Persevere*, Chile (P)
Martin, Marigold, *Silhouettes in the City*, Antigua & Barbuda (O)
Mason, Mary, *Bright Colours*, (S)
Mather, Ingrid, *Geometry*, Bangladesh (P)
Maule, Jo, *Reach for the Stars*, Palau (O)
Maunder, Eileen,
    Blue Garden, (S)
    Crazy Triangles, Hong Kong (O)
Mayhew, Azalea, *Pioneer Spirit*, Timor-Leste (P)
McCall, Maureen, *Going for Gold*, (S)
McCue, Joanne, *The Colours of Scotland*, East Timor (O)
McDonald, Rosemary, quilted by Tiddly Dyke Quilters, *Patriotic Pathways*, Rwanda (P)
McKillop, Patricia, quilted by Hannah's Room, *High Summer*, Italy (P)
McLeod, Pamela, *Kernow Inspiration*, Cyprus (P)
Millington, Jo-Ann, *Lemon Lime Fizz*, Bermuda (P)
Monins, Kim, *Goose Creek*, Pakistan (O)
Moody, Ann, *A Star is Born*, Palestine (P)
Moore, Carol and Eileen Hall, *Perseverance*, Costa Rica (P)
Moore, Margaret, *Oriental Garden*, Chinese Taipei (P)

Morgan, Joy, *Circles*, Hong Kong (P)
Morris, Edith,
    Dreaming of Roses, Samoa (P)
    Pink Roses, Turkmenistan (O)
Mowat, Carol, *Here's to You!* Jordan (P)
Muckhart Quilters, *Serendipity*, Slovenia (O)
Murray, Andrea, *Garden Reverie*, British
    Virgin Islands (O)
Murtagh, Caroline, *An Exmoor View*, Faroe
    Islands (P)

N

Nythe Patchwork & Quilting Group,
    Bright Delight, Egypt (P)
    Down our Way, Liberia (P)

O

Oakwood Quilters, *Well Dressing*,
    Micronesia (O)
Oliver, Ellen, *Rings O'Roses*, Luxembourg (O)
Osborn, Ingrid, *Peace & Freedom*, Turkey (P)
Ouse Valley Quilters Evening Group,
    Everyone's a Star, Iceland (O)
Out of Africa, quilted by Hannah's Room,
    Well Spotted, Guatemala (O)
Owl Quilters, *Flying High*, Chinese Taipei (O)

P

P & Q's Lincoln, *Lincolnshire*, Finland (P)
Panes, Sarah, *Stars of the World*, Marshall
    Islands (O)
Parker, Christine, *In The Pink*, (S)
Parry, Mary, *Blooming for Success*, Laos (P)
Parsons, Wendy, *The Raven*, Malta (O)
Patcham Patchworkers, *Floral England*,
    Malawi (O)
Patchwork Friends, *Weaving Friendships*,
    Dominican Republic (O)
Payne, Sarah, *Diving In*, Senegal (O)
Payne, Shirley, *Mirror Image*, (S)
Pearce, Anne, *On the Beach*, Bahrain (P)
Peffer, Pam,
    Nine Patch & Triangles, Papua New
    Guinea (O)
    Sampler Blocks, Bermuda (O)
Pegg, Patricia, *Caterwauling (in memory of
    Marmaduke & Pickles)*, Botswana (O)
Penny Loaf Patchers, *Pride of London*, (S)
Pentin, Jill, *Hand of Friendship*, Vietnam (P)
Perrin, Patsy, *Bright Mix*, American Samoa (P)
Phillips, Gail,
    First off the Blocks, Egypt (O)
    Pink Stars, (S)
    Spaced out on Spots, Sri Lanka (O)
Pinewood Quilters, *Friendship Star from
    London* (S)
Pontypridd Women's Institute, *Layers and
    Landmarks*, Tonga (O)
Poringland Library Quilters,
    Glorious Norfolk, Pakistan (P)
    Norfolk, UK, Puerto Rico (O)
Porter, Christine, quilted by Midsomer
    Quilting, *Twisted Mosaic*, Mongolia (O)
Postlethwaite, Eileen, *Blue Windmills*,
    Seychelles (O)

Q

Quilters Dream, *Everyone's Dreams*,
    Venezuela (P)
Quilters of All Saints Village, Axminster,
    Patriotic Pinwheels, Portugal (O)

R

Rawlins, Freda, *Around the World in 80
    Days*, San Marino (P)

Rawlins, Mary, *Circle of Friends*, Brazil (P)
Rees-Griffiths, Gwynfai, *Feathers from the
    Past*, Benin (O)
Region 13A Young Quilters, *Hands of
    Friendship*, Austria (O)
Reid, Carol, *Jack in the Box*, Singapore (P)
Richards, Di, *Beating Hearts*, Senegal (P)
Ringmer Quilters, *Variations on Around the
    World*, Turkmenistan (P)
Roberts, Joelynn, *Batik in Lines*, Central
    African Republic (O)
Roberts, Margaret, *Pinwheels*, Kenya (P)
Rodwell, Ruth, *Ohio Stars*, The Netherlands (P)
Round, Dorothy, quilted by Elisabeth Green,
    Emblems, Madagascar (P)
Rowington Quilters, *Green & Pleasant Land*,
    New Zealand (P)
Royal School of Needlework, *Opus Anglicus
    Rosarum (English Rose Work)*,
    Switzerland (O)
Royce, Kay, *Celebrations*, San Marino (O)
Rudling, Sheila,
    Corner Stripes, (S)
    Shading my Corner, (S)
    Use the Blue Stepping Stones Please!
    (S)
Rundle, Jenny, *Colours on Track*, Suriname (O)
    quilted by Jasmine Blackman, *In Transit*,
    Sweden (O)
    quilted by Mandy Parks, *Oriental
    Pizzazz*, Montenegro (P)
Russell, Hazel,
    Can you Find the Cats? Cameroon (O)
    Fantasy Flowers, St Lucia (O)
Rust, Margaret, *Norfolk Stepping Stones*,
    Panama (P)

S

1st Swanmore Brownies, *Lend a Hand*, St
    Vincent & The Grenadines (O)
Sales, Elizabeth, quilted by Lindsey Foster,
    Celebrations, Mali (O)
Sarisberie Quilters, *Jinny's Star*,
    Uzbekistan (P)
Seaford Day Group of the Ouse Valley
    Quilters, *Sussex by the Sea*, Kuwait (O)
Sedgley, Carole, quilted by Butterfly Quilting,
    Harmony, Uganda (P)
Setchell, Margaret, *Stormy Seas &
    Seashore,* (S)
Sew'n'Sews, *Mony a Mickle Maks a Muckle*,
    Nicaragua (O)
Sewell Park Q & P's, *Views of Norfolk*,
    Uzbekistan (O)
Sharman, Gill, *Town and Country*, The
    Gambia (O)
Sharp, Becky,
    Amish Purple Quilt, Panama (O)
    Touching Stars, Benin (P)
Sheffield, Aline, *Patriotic Pinwheels*,
    Democratic Republic of the Congo (P)
Shergold, Chris, *Starting Blocks*, (S)
Sherratt, Hilary, *Geometry*, North Korea (O)
Shipton Quilters, *Shipton all Stars*,
    Mauritania (O)
Shirley Quilters, *A Quilt of Many Colours*,
    Tanzania (P)
Short, Mary, quilted by Mandy Parks,
    Pleasures of Bournemouth, Cuba (O)
Sillitoe, Julia, *Flaming Stars*, Ecuador (P)
Simmonds, Pat,
    quilted by Yvette Ness, *Indigo Blues*,
    Mexico (O)
    & Jenny Rundle, *Blue Iris*, The
    Netherlands (O)

Simpson, Juliet, *Made for You*, Yemen (O)
Simpson, Pat, *Weaving Amongst the Stars*,
    Jordan (O)
Simpson, Peter, *Crazy Collection of
    Gentlemen's Ties*, El Salvador (O)
Skinner, Gill, *Starting Point*, Peru (P)
Smith, Barbara,
    Chequers, Austria (P)
    Squares & Crosses, Botswana (P)
Smith, Joy & Joyce Lewns,
    Garden of England, Gabon (O)
    Whitstable by the Sea, Honduras (O)
Smith, Sue, *Memories of my Father P F
    DeBoerr*, Togo (O)
Snell, Meta,
    Around the Square, Comoros (O)
    Land and Sea, Puerto Rico (P)
    Stars in Tilting Squares, Lesotho (O)
Sommerville, Janet, *Crossing the Border*,
    Nigeria (P)
Soroptimist International of Kidderminster &
    District Club, *Garden of Friendship*,
    Bosnia & Herzegovina (P)
Sowells, Jan, quilted by Helen Elgar,
    Crossing the Line, Kazakhstan (P)
Spargo, Ann, *Stars all Round*, Sao Tome &
    Principe (O)
Springbank Quilters, *Wonderful
    Worcestershire*, Qatar (O)
St Mary's Convent & Nursing Home (Craft
    Group), *Through the Square Window*,
    Belgium (O)
Stacey, Ann, *Morris Dancing*, Afghanistan
    (O)
Stamp, Ann, *All Around the World*, Brunei
    (O)
Stitchmates, *Flags of Friendship*, Belarus (O)
Stockbridge, Celia, *Big Red Buses*,
    Lithuania (P)
Stone, Denise, *Hearts* (S)
Stuart, Elizabeth, *Lightning Stars*, Djibouti
    (O)

T

Test Valley Quilters,
    quilted by The Cotton Patch, *An English
    Dawn*, Ukraine (P)
    quilted by Fir Tree Quilting, *Around the
    World with Sybil*, Japan (P)
    quilted by Izzy Hall, *Circles Around the
    World*, Cape Verde (P)
    quilted by Sue Sapstead, *Circles of
    Hope*, Macao (P)
    quilted by Compton Quilting Services,
    Colours of Wessex, Czechoslovakia
    Republic (O)
    quilted by Janie Rowthorn, *Crossing
    Borders*, Bosnia- Herzegovina (O)
    quilted by Kath Allaway, *London Meets
    the World*, South Korea (P)
    quilted by Sheila Wilkinson, *Podium
    Steps*, Brunei (P)
    quilted by The Cotton Patch, *Shades of
    Klee*, Croatia (O)
    quilted by Karen Cocksedge, *Tree of Life*,
    Zambia (O)
    quilted by The Cotton Patch, *Weymouth
    & Portland Wave to the World*, Ireland
    (O)
Testwood Quilters,
    All Buttoned Up, Lebanon (O)
    Crazy for You, Thailand (P)
The London and Middlesex Region of the
    Quilters' Guild, *British Butterflies*,
    Liechtenstein (P)

The Nuneaton Crop, *Serendipity*, Finland (O)

The Pumpkin Patchers, *Union Stars*, Bahamas (O)

The Quirky Quilters Burscough & District U3A, *Rhapsody in Blue*, Mozambique (O)

The Sarajevo Quilters, *International Stars*, Hungary (O)

Thomas, Pat, *Bow Ties & Pearly Kings & Queens*, Slovakia (P)

Three Shires Quilters, *The Three Shires*, Macedonia (P)

Tiddly Dyke Quilters, quilted by Mandy Park, *Sports at The Games,* Project Logo Quilt quilted by Midsomer Quilting, *Peace and Liberty*, Haiti (O)

Tillingbourne Valley Stitchers, *Londinium MMXII*, Cambodia (P)

Tooze, Michelle, *Hopes, Dreams & Successful Teams*, Poland (P)

Tooze, Susan, *Good Luck & Success*, Haiti (P)

Totley Brook Quilters, *Sporting Sheffield*, The Philippines (O)

Tremlett, Rosemary, *Spring*, Papua New Guinea (P)

Tremlett, Sandy, *Mosaics*, Albania (O)

Tritton, Sally, *Surrounded by Sea*, Kyrgyzstan (P)

Tunbridge Wells Quilters, *The Village*, Cote-d'Ivoire (O)

Turner, Janet & Carol Barton, *Purrfect Cats*, Croatia (P)

Twigg, Patricia, *Mabel's Dream*, Iran (O)

U

U3A Stroud, *Jazzy Stroud*, Liechtenstein (O)

Underhill, Ann, *Dancing Around the World*, Aruba (O)

Urry, Jan, *The Geese Fly Home*, Niger (O)

Uxbridge High School with Elisabeth Green, *Team Effort*, Estonia (P)

W

1st West Horndean Rainbows, Brownies & Guides, *Guiding Around the World*, Canada (P)

Walker, Alvine, *United in Sport*, Chile (O)

Walker, Gail, *Good Luck*, Central African Republic (P)

Walker, Vera, *Skewed Green & Sunlight*, Maldives (O)

Waterside Quilters, *Island of Dreams*, Turkey (O)

Watters, Sue, *Stars United*, Mozambique (P)

Webb, Patricia,
A Green and Pleasant Land, Belarus (P)
London Calling, Gabon (P)

Wessex Quiltmakers,
Hands Around the World, Laos (O)
Hands of Friendship, Norway (P)

West Wight Quilters, *By the Seaside*, Guyana (O)

Westrop, Barbara, *Stars Among the Flowers*, Bhutan (O)

Wheatley, Dorothy & Elisabeth Green, *My Home Town*, Congo (O)

Wheeler, Elizabeth, *London Challenge*, Indonesia (P)

Whitney, June, *The Green Hills of Home*, Namibia (O)

Wild, Linda, *Running Wild LDN*, Kazakhstan (O)

Windmill Quilters, *Wind in Your Sails*, Suriname (P)

Wing, Hazel, *Formation Flying*, Djibouti (P)

Wombourne Quilters, *Around Wombourne in 2011*, Equatorial Guinea (O)

Women's Have A Go Group, *Have a Go*, Nepal (O)

Wooller, Margaret, *Long Life & Harmony*, Qatar (P)

Woolley, Debbie, *Scraps of Red & Gold Dust*, South Korea (O)

Wycherley, Jane, *Cottage Garden*, Sweden (P)

Y

Young, Ann, *Varying Pathways*, Cayman Islands (O)

Young, Eve & Elisabeth Green, *English Garden*, Guinea-Bissau (O)

Acknowledgements

A Gift of Quilts would like to thank the following:

Individuals, Groups and Organisations

Kaffe Fassett
Brandon Mably
Mary Short – the third member of the project team
David Matthews – photographer
Tony Oliver - photographer
Elisabeth Green – for finishing so many tops
Andrew Salmon, Twisted Threads Exhibitions
Marilyn Lovett – President of The Quilters' Guild of the British Isles
Tiddly Dyke Quilters - Andover
Coats Crafts UK
Goose Chase Quilting
Christine Porter
The Quilters' Guild of the British Isles
Francesca Canty – UK & International Cultural Programme and Partnerships Manager
The Rt Hon Sir George Young Bt MP
Mark D. Hyland, President/CEO Handi Quilter Inc.
Amy Butler

Long Arm Quilters

Mandy Parks, The Quilt's Whiskers
Janie Rowthorn, Oakleaf Quilting
Jasmine Blackman
Sheila Wilkinson
Julie Barnes
Susie Green, Duxhurst Quilting
Kath Allaway, The Silver Thimble
Sue Sapstead, Quiltessence
Yvette Ness, Needles and Threads
Karen Cocksedge, Karens Quilts
Karen Florey, Running Chicken
Liz Sewell, The Cotton Patch
Claire Tinsley's, Hannah's Room
Tracey Pereira, Teepee Quilts
Barbara Sutcliffe, Fir Tree Quilting
Twambley Quilted by Jude
Midsomer Quilting

The team, Jenny Rundle, Mary Short & Sharon Garrick with Kaffe Fassett & Brandon Mably

We would like to thank all of you who have helped us in many ways too numerous to mention, but you know who you are. Thank You.

ENJOY A RANGE OF CRAFT MAGAZINES